William Kotzwinkle is the author of such cult classics as *The Fan Man*, *Doctor Rat*, *Swimmer in the Secret Sea*, *Jack in the Box*, *Fata Morgana* and other highly acclaimed and successful works.

He has twice won the National Magazine Award for Fiction and has won the World Fantasy Award.

He lives in the United States of America and has worked as cook, chauffeur, lumberjack – and as a department store Santa Claus.

William Kotzwinkle

CHRISTMAS AT FONTAINE'S

First published in Great Britain by
Andre Deutsch Ltd 1983
Published in Abacus by
Sphere Books Ltd 1984
30–32 Gray's Inn Road, London WC1X 8JL
Copyright © 1982 by William Kotzwinkle

Printed and bound in Great Britain by
Cox & Wyman Ltd, Reading

SOMETHING FUNNY was going on in Fontaine's Department Store. Officer Locke, security guard of thirty-five years' experience, rode the escalator from floor to floor, eyes darting about suspiciously. In Ladies Lingerie, he paused; the cold stare that swept through the aisle caused the women browsing there to look around for the shoplifter in their ranks. Had someone tucked a girdle in her purse? Locke proceeded slowly up the aisle, like a bear looking for lunch, and quite innocent shoppers grew uneasy, and retired to the dressing rooms until he was gone.

'Locke's at it again.' At the heart of the store's security system, Locke's image flashed on a bank of tv surveillance screens. The guard monitoring the screens could see customers growing nervous, fanning out, fading, a wave of paranoia rippling along from screen to screen, where Locke's heavy plodding figure moved.

'Look like the secon' floor of Sing Sing prison roun' here,' said a second guard, at the other end of the monitoring bank, as

1

the wave came his way along the screens. 'Ole Locke puttin' the *chill* on folks.'

'He told me,' said the first guard, 'that somebody's been hiding in the store at night.'

'Somebody hidin' in Locke's hat.' This guard, an elderly gentleman who'd known Chester Locke a long time, was convinced that Locke was deranged. He'd watched him for years, Locke going at his job like a crazed ape, especially when it came to throwing children out of the store. Security Guard Galloway Jones had seen Locke shake little troublemakers until their teeth rattled, and then fling them into the street. Once, Officer Jones had watched stupified as Locke held two ten-year-old hooligans over an open elevator shaft, letting them stare in terror into its dark grinding depths for about twenty seconds, until their hair was standing on end. Then he threw them out of the store.

'... so if you ast me,' Officer Jones said now, 'Locke jus' out of his *mind*.'

Locke mounted the next escalator and rode upward, his own head a delicate surveillance device, scanning, fine-focusing, picking up little details the ordinary eye overlooks. And in each department, he saw traces of an alien presence, one that was gliding behind the scenes at night, leaving a faint trail wherever it went.

Locke rode off the top step of the escalator into Sporting Goods. The glass eyes of a stuffed moosehead gazed down at him, electronically relaying another picture of Locke to the command center, along with the image of a small, ragged urchin who was quietly playing in the aisle with a new baseball glove, bending down as if to catch a hot grounder. In the next moment he was dangling in the air at the end of Locke's arm; in the moment following that he was stumbling onto the down escalator, tears in his eyes, and the imprint of Locke's size 14 shoe on his hindmost past.

'Man be secon' cousin to a rhinoc'rous,' said Galloway Jones, nodding toward Locke's image on his screen, and to that of the sobbing ragamuffin descending on the escalator. 'Those kids ain't got no toys and they sure ain't gonna git none fo' Christmas, so they come and play in the store. What's wrong with that? Why ole Locke hafta be so mean about it?'

'I think,' said Officer Jones' partner, 'a kid musta bit him once.'

'Mo' likely Locke bit the chile,' said Officer Jones.

Locke stalked back through Sporting Goods, past a row of big-game rifles with scope attached. His own career boasted many trophies, including professional shoplifters wearing false hats, shoes, and coats with special linings. But his greatest pleasure seemed to come from holding the front door of the store open and flipping underprivileged children into the street.

If we had a scanning device to scan memory, we might run it over Chester Locke's, in an attempt to find out why he is so cranky, especially at Christmas time. There would be pictures of his own childhood perhaps, spent in Hell's Kitchen and including a shot of Chester's tanked-up father performing the regular Christmas ceremony—throwing the tree, ornaments and all, through the front window. This, and other revealing sequences would help us to understand, but it wouldn't soften Locke's soul one bit. And something funny is going on in the store.

He exited Sporting Goods and stepped onto the next escalator, as if crags and ledges were above him, leading to slopes where rare quarry bounded nimbly. Locke went up like a packing crate, inert, dumb, heavy; but his surveillance system was humming.

'Ho, ho, ho! Merry Christmas!' This from Santa Claus, enthroned in the distance—for Locke had reached Toyland. He stood fast, examining the aisles, and the children. His menacing gaze caused them to hide behind their mothers' skirts, or simply break into tears. Even the stuffed animals on

3

the shelves seemed to huddle together under his withering stare. An icy wind had entered the department and it was unrelated to North Pole Headquarters, where Santa sat amidst his elves, entertaining the children.

'Ho, ho, ho ...'

Locke snorted under his breath as he gazed at Santa's territory—a snow-covered cottage with reindeer on the roof and elves in the wintry front yard, the entire thing surrounded by a white picket fence. Locke didn't care for the arrangement, never had. The fenced yard, the staircase to Santa's throne, the snow-covered cottage—they cut off the entire back corner of the floor, turning it into a shoplifter's sanctuary.

Locke shuffled on by North Pole Headquarters, resentful of every cardboard brick of it. His revolver creaked in its holster; the children whimpered and drew back, perhaps thinking he might fire on them, or lead them like lemmings into an open shaft. Children know—they can tell who loves them and who doesn't. Their ranks pressed nearer to Santa, and farther from Locke—the two uniformed figures like balanced weights on the scales of human feelings.

'Ho, ho, ho,' said Santa, and Locke emitted a grunt, or a growl, some rough guttural sound in any case, which shuddered through the children. He was looking at the huge piled-up sleigh on the roof of the cottage, into which mechanical elves were placing toys, again and again, filling it, filling it—while behind the cottage any amateur could be pocketing a three-hundred dollar video game, unseen, and impossible to collar.

Worse than that—somebody was hiding in the store.

Just last night that person had been in Toyland, this Locke knew, and it was making him exceedingly grouchy. But no jazzbo could slip by Chester Locke for long, that was certain; he'd make a mistake soon enough, and Locke would grab him.

A door in the rear of Toyland opened and Herbert Muhlstock the department manager emerged, clipboard in hand. Like Locke, he seemed to have a deep loathing for children. The department had done this to him, with its shelves always in disarray and so much of the stock damaged by children before it could be sold. He struck with his pencil at the clipboard, as if assigning those children in the near aisle to forced labor in uninhabitable climates.

Locke joined him at the shelves. 'Somebody's hiding in the store.'

'Oh?' Muhlstock turned. 'Where?'

'Maybe here.'

'It wouldn't surprise me.' Muhlstock looked at the children, his face undergoing a nervous tic. 'They're liable to try anything.'

'You seen anything funny?'

'There—' Muhlstock pointed to a small child on tip-toe before a performing music box, a child whose innocence was pure snow falling on unblemished ground; with tiny hands it clumsily wound the key, and then, with blissful smile watched enraptured the fairy dance within the box. 'You're looking for trouble, there it is right in front of us.'

Muhlstock moved on, surveying the ruin of his department at this, the worst time of the year. His hand shook; a vein in his temple bulged. He loved order, neat stacks of things, stability in general. Toyland was a house of cards, always collapsing, and it was slowly giving him a nervous breakdown. He was unsuited for the work, should be elsewhere in the store, but who of us ever lands where we'd like to be?

A child danced by, tossing pieces of a gameboard around, scattering the pieces at Muhlstock's feet, Muhlstock, a man whose every pencil must be perfectly aligned on his desk, whose paperclips form compulsive polyhedrons of mystical significance. Is it surprising that his face now began to twitch violently?

Muhlstock twitched, and Locke continued his rounds, back down the escalator. In Hardware he lifted a pair of street kids in the air and shook them until their shoelaces came untied and the hammer and saw they'd been playing with had been dropped in terror. Then he dragged them toward the freight elevator. When it opened, he flung them inside it, so that they bounced off the padded wall with a dull thud.

The freight operator looked at them, then Locke. 'Down?'

'And out,' growled Locke, and the doors closed.

He stalked on.

WINIFRED INGRAM, pouring boiling water through coffee-filter cones until she was ready to drop, dropped finally, and closed up the Miracle Filter display counter at five to nine. She'd served coffee samples all day, and had drunk so much coffee herself, her nerves were like an electrified fence.

'I've had it,' she said to the woman behind her, who'd spent the day slicing cheese, lettuce, onions and part of her finger on a gadget imported from Italy, The woman, Mrs. Gomez, pointed a bandaged finger at the slicer. 'You know who made this? Mussolini's nephew.'

On all sides of them, other culinary demonstration booths were closing, and the atmosphere of the store was changing, a single image seeming to float in everyone's mind—that of soaking feet.

'I'm so wired,' said Winifred, unplugging her hot place, 'I feel like robbing a bank.'

'Why don't we switch tomorrow,' suggested Mrs. Gomez. 'I'll make coffee, you slice fingers.'

An adenoidal voice sounded over the loudspeakers:
'ADDENSHUN, SHOBBERS, DA STORE ID NOW CLOSING ...'

'Laurence Olivier,' said Mrs. Gomez, throwing her leftover onion slices in a garbage bag.

'He's Mr. Fontaine's brother-in-law,' said Winifred.

'He's Mussolini's nephew,' said Mrs. Gomez, and trudged heavily out from behind her booth, toward the employees' exit, to punch the time clock and go home. Winifred Ingram spent a last few nervous minutes arranging her coffee counter for the next day's caffeine jag, to be shared by thousands. Ears pounding, blood pressure rocketing, she slipped out from the Miracle Filter counter. Working behind it was no joy, but last year she'd demonstrated perfume and reeked for the season; when people beside her in the elevator grew dizzy she began referring to the scent as Agent Orange, and had been reprimanded by her supervisor.

Now she walked on tender toes toward the locker room, a cheerless cinderblock wing filling rapidly with tired, crazed, and suicidal colleagues.

'... my hair feels like cardboard ...'

'... I wanted to scream in her face but I just started crying ...'

'... perfect stranger asked me to dinner and I said yes and gave him my phone number only now I think he must be a psychopath, what do you think ...'

Winifred opened her locker, took out her overcoat and hat, and punched the time clock. The nasty little machine clicked at her, stamping the hour. The final humiliation came at the door, where the Security Chief personally inspected everyone's pocketbook for stolen merchandise. Winifred plopped hers down under his gaze.

He pointed coldly. 'Open it.'

'Oh, I hope,' said Winifred softly to the girl beside her, 'he doesn't find the vacuum cleaner.' The girl, dazed from giftwrapping packages for twelve straight hours, stared back

8

dumbly. Winifred patted her shoulder. 'Go right home and hang from the door frame.'

'Hey lady,' said the Security Chief, 'there are people behind you.' He shoved her pocketbook toward her.

'You mean you don't want my gold fillings?'

'Very funny.'

'... and my eyeglasses ...' Winifred snapped her pocketbook closed and stumbled forward. Really, she thought, I've got to shut up, but the caffeine was raging in her brain, twenty-five cups of coffee loosening speech centers she didn't know she had. Mumbling to herself, she went out the door, into the storm. Mrs. Gomez was standing at the curb, waiting for the cross-town bus. Winifred waved to her and Mrs. Gomez waved back, with bandaged fingers.

Winifred proceeded along the avenue with the crowds that were enjoying the window displays of mechanical toys performing—elves, fairies, brightly costumed animals. She moved gayly, talking to strangers. '... isn't it marvelous ... don't you just love the elephant ...'

I'm burning my reserves, she thought. I'm going to be dishwater in about an hour. '... oh, that dancing mouse is such a darling ...'

It wasn't just the twenty-five cups of coffee, of course. It was the loneliness of the holidays, when her kids went off to their father. Why had she ever allowed that concession? Why hadn't she flirted with the judge? The children would be home tonight if she had. Instead she was chattering to a little bald-headed man about a mechanical bear riding a toy bicycle across a tightrope. 'Oh, don't you hope he doesn't fall off?'

The man edged away from her, and she caught a momentary glimpse of herself in the window glass, hat jammed on sideways, hair askew, eyes protruding. Winifred, for god's sake, calm down, before you go into orbit.

She slipped out of the window crowd, back into the sidewalk flow, contenting herself with some off-key caroling under her breath. Snowflakes fell all around her, and she wondered what it was like tonight at the house in Connecticut, which she'd gayly liberated herself from. The kids would be snuggled up with their father, possibly by the tree, possibly eating fruit cake, possibly under the tender, calculating gaze of one of Bob's new girlfriends.

But, thought Winifred, at this time of good will I wish them well. The girlfriend could be stricken with incurable hiccups, but that's all.

Incurable hiccups and *maybe* a mild stroke. Other than that she should live and be happy.

With my husband.

Winifred trudged along, hating Christmas, with its stupid songs and horrible melancholy. Life was difficult enough in midtown Manhattan, without all this heart-breaking cheer.

I T WAS HOT inside the enormous beard and wig, and Santa Claus had a rash from ear to ear. The two queen-sized foam pillows surrounding his midsection had turned his red uniform into a steam bath and his shiny black boots were so tight his toes were bent under with cramps.

'Ho, ho, ho ...'

He turned back the cuff of his furry sleeve and slipped a look at his watch. 'Alright, little girl, step on up here ...'

'I'm not a little girl.'

'No, of course you're not.' Santa parted the long sheepdog curls of his wig, in order to see better, but they all looked alike, especially in snowsuits. 'Well, what do you want for Christmas?'

'A submachine gun.'

'Yes, alright, and what else?'

'A real hand grenade.'

'And what are you going to do with that?'

'Throw it at my sister.'

'Well now, Santa will have to think about that one ...'

11

'She's always taking my toys.'

Santa bounced the boy on his knee. 'But maybe you should just take a few of *her* toys instead of throwing a hand grenade at her.'

'I don't like her toys. I like *my* toys.'

'Well, what sort of toys do you want me to bring you this year?'

'A real hand grenade.'

Santa set the boy down, and stood up. The line was finished, the night over. 'Time to put the reindeer to bed.'

'... and a tear-gas bomb ...' The little mercenary followed Santa across the white yard of North Pole Headquarters. Santa ushered himself and the boy out through the picket fence.

'... and a 12,000 volt rattlesnake prod ...'

Santa walked toward the freight elevator, the boy following him, tugging on Santa's pants leg.

'... and a blowgun with poisoned darts. Can you get me that?'

Santa pressed the elevator bell, his pants leg still snapping in the little fist.

'Can you? Huh?'

'When I fly over the Amazon.'

'What's the Amazon?'

The elevator opened and Santa stepped in. 'Be a good boy. Be nice to your sister.'

'How about a rubber hammer that doesn't leave any—'

The door closed on the youth's request, and the elevator sank down through the building. Santa leaned back against the padded wall and sighed into his beard. The elevator deposited him in the subbasement of the store, in a room he shared with a dozen naked manikins.

He hung his red cap on a manikin's gracefully extended wooden finger and sat down at a damaged dressing table, a cracked mirror in front of him. He removed the wig and beard. A craggy face appeared, covered in gray stubble; the traveling

12

bags beneath the eyes had seen a lot of road. When the red uniform and its two queen-size pillows came off, Santa became a thin, stoop-shouldered old drifter, his hair gray, his fingers stained with the nicotine of a million butt-ends. He lit up now, and the hand that held the weed was leathery, and shaking slightly from nerves shot long ago.

He reached under the dressing table and brought out a battered valise. He flipped the latch and opened it; a beaten-up flask was nestled there, from which he took a long swig.

Fortified, he removed his boots. '... little bitty boots like that.' He held one up and shook his head. 'Enough to make a man cry.' He tossed them in the corner, and then hung the rest of his uniform on the outstretched hands and elbows of the wooden ladies.

'Don't let no one pinch it, girls.' He put on his street clothes—a faded work shirt, old jeans and a navy peacoat. 'But if they want those boots, they can help themselves.'

He turned off the light and left, out through the sub-basement, toward the employees' exit. The security guards waved him through, no one having the heart to search Santa—they knew him from previous years, the old hobo who always showed up at Christmas, never said much, and went his way afterwards.

Now he stepped out onto the avenue and turned the corner, stopping to look at the windows of the store, where his counterpart, a mechanical Santa in antique costume was driving a Victorian sled across a mechanical sky—stars drifting by, and moon, and Milky Way.

Santa continued along in the crowd, from window to window, each one fantastic, with toy figures dancing, jumping through hoops, skating on glass. But the center window on the avenue, just past the big main doors, was covered by a heavy red curtain. They were late getting that one set up; nobody'd seen it yet. The grapevine said it was electrical problems, the whole shebang didn't want to dance, or bow, or whatever it was supposed to do. Too bad, because it was probably quite the window, probably the best one of all.

'Hurry it up there, boys,' said Santa softly as he passed. 'Christmas is almost here.'

Behind the curtain stood Dann Sardos, studying the problem—a make-believe village inhabited by mechanical animals. The animals held the foreground of the window, and in back of them was a row of odd-shaped gingerbread houses, tilted, dreamlike; beyond the houses was a painted backdrop that showed a distant mountain range, faintly visible through painted clouds.

'It doesn't make it,' said Sardos.

'It's beautiful,' said his assistant, Jeff Beck. 'Pull the curtain.'

'We've stalled this long,' said Sardos. 'We might as well get it right.'

'Right? It *is* right.' Beck stroked the head of a large reindeer and talked soothingly to the beast. 'Your tail goes up and down. Your eyes light. But Sardos is never satisfied.'

'Shut up,' said Sardos softly.

'Don't be nervous,' said Beck. 'We'll get it done—by Easter.'

The reindeer was parked outside a building marked Airport, at the end of the village street, far left in the window. Inside the Airport were fixed wooden figures of elves, weighing luggage marked *Santa Claus*. Beside the Airport was the village Inn, and next to it a General Store, then a Laundromat, and a Tea Shoppe, all of them big enough to admit a grown child or a desperate art director. Dann Sardos knelt in the street and shook his head. 'The Inn isn't saying anything.'

'Yes, it is,' said Beck. 'It's saying, please Dann, pull the curtain.' Beck turned toward Sardos. 'May I remind you there are only three more shopping days until Christmas?'

'I'm way past caring.'

Beck seemed to sag, back toward the Airport reindeer. 'Your

14

antlers glow. But Sardos doesn't want anybody to see you. Why? WHY, WHY, WHY?'

'Calm down,' said Sardos. 'We've got to do something with this Inn, otherwise it's just dead space.'

Jeff Beck swayed gently toward Sardos with his claw hammer, lifting it in slow motion as would a mechanical toy, in order to hit Sardos over the head with it. 'Give up, Dann. For the sake of our future in the business, I beg you—pull the curtain.'

'Not yet. I think I'm about to have a new inspiration.'

'Nobody's *paying* you for anymore inspiration. Who do you think you are—Pablo Picasso?'

The street of the village was slotted, to permit the animals to move in various directions, controlled by traveling levers and dollies that tracked beneath the floor. All sections of the floor were hinged, and Sardos had lifted one of the sections now, studying the intricate nest of electrical contacts fixed to it.

Beck pointed with his hammer. 'Don't fool with the panel again, Dann. That way leads to madness. You'll pull it apart and it'll take me a day to put it back together, a day we don't have. Every Christmas display in the city has been going for weeks. Except ours.'

'Every day we don't open this window,' said Sardos, 'more people come around, wondering what's in it.'

'Wondering what's in your *head*. Wondering—' Beck moved the hammer, again in slow motion. '—wondering why you are such a nit-picking, never-satisfied egotistical *screwball*.'

He tossed the hammer down, and spun in slow pantomime, toward three other inhabitants of the village, the Three Little Pigs, whose hands were joined in a ring outside the Laundromat. Beck threw the main control switch and the Three Little Pigs started to turn in a circle, Beck turning with them. 'Why, why, why won't he finish his window, Little Pigs? Why won't he let them see you dance ...'

15

The whole village was moving now, electrical motors and belts humming softly beneath the floor, animating a dashing Wolf in feathered cap who was creeping up on the Pigs; further down the street, at the village square, a pair of dogs were playing cards with an elegant skunk, her great fluffy tail moving slowly back and forth.

In front of the Tea Shoppe, as if about to enter it, were a pair of white lady hares in white fur capes, their long ears turning this way and that. The only human figure in the village was Pinocchio, who stood at the end of the street, looking into it, his nose growing longer, then shorter, then longer again.

'The whole thing isn't—radical enough,' said Sardos.

'What are you anyway!' screamed Beck. 'A revolutionary? Have you kidnapped us? Me—' He whirled with his hammer, pointing, '—and the Bunny Sisters?'

Sardos had moved to the end of the street, where he stood in front of Pinocchio. 'We've got to shift the enchanted boy. He's lost down here.'

Beck charged after him. 'It's three days before Christmas. It's time to call it a night, Dann. Throw in your test-light, sign your name at the bottom, and let me PULL THE CURTAIN!'

'Relax,' said Sardos. 'I know what I'm doing.'

'If only you did,' said Beck. 'But you don't. I haven't bought a single gift for a friend, relative, or enemy. Why? Because I spend all my waking hours working on this—*nightmare*— window of yours.'

'I know what's wrong with the reindeer,' said Sardos. 'I know why he appears static.'

'... no ...' sobbed Beck. '... no, no, no ...'

'I want his tail to light up, with Santa's signature. S—A—N—T—A.'

'I know how to spell,' said Beck. 'Do you know how long it will take me to do that?'

'Forever.'

'Until St. Valentine's Day, anyway. At which time won't it

look odd, a reindeer's tail lighting up with hello Santa on it?'

'Time is relative.'

'Time is M—O—N—E—Y. Why don't we have our reindeer spell that with his tail?'

'Proceed.' Sardos pointed to the reindeer's tail.

'Dann, what if Louis Fontaine fires us? You know when sales are down, he fires people. Why shouldn't he fire you and me? We could be walking the streets tomorrow. And jobs like this are hard to find. In fact, there aren't any. I know because I've been looking for one. To get away from you. If we blow it, we'll end up at the Warren Street Employment Agency, signing on as dishwashers.'

'Did you know,' said Sardos, 'that someone is hiding in the store at night?'

'No, I didn't. Are they from the Internal Revenue Service? I hear they're after Louis Fontaine, which is another reason he's firing people.'

'It was after midnight last night when I left. I saw a shadow moving through the aisles.'

'It's the Ghost of Christmas Past,' said Beck, 'of which this window is a part.'

'This is the window of the future,' said Sardos.

'It's just a bunch of toy animals, Dann. Can't you understand? It's lollipop land. Who *cares* what you do here? It's a dead myth.'

'Never say die,' said Sardos.

LOUIS FONTAINE, by night, remained in the store, a captain who could not sleep while the bountiful ocean of Christmas was being sailed. Except this year it felt like the Dead Sea.

Fontaine sat in his richly appointed office, looking at the day's sales figures. His eyebrows had narrowed into a frown. He reached in his coat pocket for a cigar, and finding it empty, crossed the office to a 17th century walnut bureau, from which he removed a handful. Moments later, a rare Persian carpet received cigar ash in its weave, as Fontaine paced the office, deep in thought. The office had been created by Dann Sardos, from art auctions at Sotheby's. There were Federal marble tables, and Victorian mahogany chests, graced by continental glass, ceramics, and silver. There was an 18th-century Dutch clock, with wheels of gilded brass upon its face, showing configurations of the moon; but it was the wheel of days Louis Fontaine was gazing at, the wheel that showed him but Three More Shopping Days Until Christmas.

Again he frowned, then crossed the carpet once more, to the

far wall. There he opened a sliding teakwood panel, and the sleeping store appeared below—rows and rows of quality merchandise.

'Buy,' he said quietly into the air. He raised his arms. 'Buy, buy, buy.'

He closed the sliding panel, clicked off his Empire light, and left the office.

He walked down the executive hallway, past darkened office doors, to the employee staircase. He descended, entering the store, into Men's Wear.

'Buy,' he intoned through the dark aisles. 'Buy lots, buy all!'

Manikins were mounted on pedestals, in the suits and topcoats of the season, their painted eyes gazing into the deeper distances of the store, where Fontaine's own gaze traveled. 'I'll hold you together with my bare hands,' he said to the great collection of goods. 'I'll sell you myself if I have to. For I can sell stockings to amputees. *I can sell anything.*'

Relief seemed to come to him after this outburst. Nonetheless, tragic discounts were being offered all around him. He handled a pair of men's briefs. 'At this price no man should be without new underpants.'

Underpants, a nice Christmas gift, were not moving. Neither were socks and ties. Had the spirit of Christmas died? He held the package of briefs in the air. 'Designer underpants. You'll never see them at this price again.' He flipped the package back on the shelf, and walked on.

Buy, buy, buy. Buy something, buy anything.

He tried to encompass the entire tangle of the store's merchandise in his mind, but it was impossible. He had so much now, it took roomfuls of college morons to count it for him. He'd fire them all tomorrow.

He relit his cigar and walked on, smoke streaming behind him. At the escalator, he turned and walked down it, toward the next floor. Sale signs hung on the wall, their edges ornamented with fine calligraphic designs. 'My advertising staff,' said Fontaine, in a harsh whisper. 'I'll fire them too. I'll fire *everybody*. Except myself.'

He envisioned clones of Louis Fontaine at every counter, selling the right way. Through *magnetism*.

He entered Bathroom Articles—cabinets, carpets, ensembles. His voice echoed among the tubs, as he stared at a pair of grotesque gold-plated sink fixtures.

'What incredible fool brought these into this store?'

He puffed angrily on his cigar. A faint memory stirred.

I did. In my Venetian period.

I must have been nuts, nobody will buy faucets like these. They look like Nazi hood ornaments. Hermann Goering I could sell them to.

But not to Mr. and Mrs. New York City.

A flashlight beam suddenly burst upon him. 'Oh—sorry, sir.' A gravelly voice came from beyond the beam. 'I didn't know you were still in the store.'

'Is that you, Locke? Take that infernal beam out of my eyes.'

Locke lowered the light, and the two men met in the aisle. Louis Fontaine looked thoughtfully for a moment at his security guard. 'People are not buying the way they used to, Locke.'

'No sir.'

'We need to stimulate sales.'

'Yessir.'

'My chauffeur is parked outside, reading Dostoevski. I am in here, losing a fortune.'

Fontaine walked on, Locke accompanying him, down through the store, from escalator to escalator, to the main floor. Eventually they came to the front of the building and to the locked door leading to Dann Sardos' window. 'Are you aware of what's going on beyond this door?' asked Fontaine. 'Has the joker let anybody in yet?'

'Not that I know of, sir.'

'Here is a terrible admission, Officer Locke, which I make to you in my own store because it is night and we're alone. I myself don't know what's going on in this window.'

The two men studied the sealed entrance. Fontaine punched the air with his cigar. 'That window is free advertising space, Locke. Space I've denied myself for four weeks, at the height of the season.'

'I heard they're having trouble with the machinery.'

'I'm firing them tomorrow.'

'Yessir.' Locke did not want to be fired. But if he didn't find whoever was hiding in the store he would be fired. Because Mr. Fontaine was in a firing mood. Locke thought:

If I lose this job I could wind up in a grocery store, guarding the meat department, where it is cold.

He vowed to himself this would not happen to Chester Locke.

Fontaine pointed with his cigar end, at the door. 'Give me your pistol, Locke. I'm going to shoot off the hinges.'

Officer Locke, every ready to obey all matters of company policy, reached for his revolver. But Louis Fontaine turned, and walked on, a trail of cigar smoke behind him.

Buy, buy, buy.

Buy expensive, buy cheap.

But buy.

MAD AGGIE walked the streets of New York, a white-haired old zany, with a shopping bag in each hand. The music of the stores blared at her from all directions, and the crowds of shoppers brushed on past her, as she shuffled along in her galoshes, talking to herself.

'It must be Christmas,' she said, her dense fog of nutty thoughts parting slightly, through which she saw a little piece of reality again—season and place, time and the human dream.

'Yes,' said Winifred Ingram, shuffling wearily herself, 'it certainly is.'

The clouds of madness closed again, and Aggie walked slowly on in her delirium, shopping bags dragging. Old newspapers and other trash protruded from the bags—Aggie's treasure, all that she had scoured from a day's search in the city. What was she searching for? A bite to eat, and something she'd lost long ago, her mind.

She raved along, fists clenched around the cord handles of her bags. The Port Authority building was ahead, buses and commuters streaming into it, as into a great mouth in a canyon wall. Aggie entered fearfully, as she entered all places, and dragged her bags across the floor, toward a bench.

She flopped onto it, bags between her short legs, and took out a slice of pizza somebody'd thrown in a garbage can. Aggie dined, and rested, trying to look like a person waiting for her bus to come.

She slumped forward on the bench, her hands loosening a little on her shopping bags, but never fully opening. Somebody might steal them.

Her eyes closed; broken images cascaded over her, edged in feverish wavering light. Heads became flames, and the hands that gestured toward her sent ripples of heat and mirage, dreams within dreams, sulfurous and burning. She saw a Christmas tree, jagged-edged, aflame, and seated around it a family, their heads haloed with the same restless fire.

The family talked, smiled, and moved about beneath the tree, and Aggie felt a little twinge, and a tugging in her mind.

The woman of fire was helping a little boy hang ornaments on the burning tree, and then some relations came, and they hung ornaments too. Aggie shifted on her bench, huddling deeper into her coat, trying to sleep, but the broken, burning images kept coming, like a movie that skipped and jumped, some of it backward, some upside-down. The woman lifted the boy to the top of the tree, to place a pointed star, and Aggie felt the twinge again, and moaned.

Was that me, was that me?

The star burst into flame, arcs of feverish light descending from it, covering relations and family; they continued to laugh and open presents, but their figures were fading behind the sheet of fire, and disappearing. The movie ended, broken, flickering off to blackness, and Aggie slept, as the crowds of commuters swirled around her.

'... ok lady, let's go, this ain't a hotel ...'

A cop was nudging her with a nightstick. She nodded, before he did worse, and she stood, clutching her bags. The building

23

echoed with voices, announcements, music. It was still early. She'd have to find another place to sleep. She dragged across the floor, bags trailing, and pushed back out, into the winter night.

OFFICER LOCKE watched through the store window as Mr. Fontaine departed in his limousine. Then Locke turned, back into the store. It was dark and completely silent now. He was alone in its spacious depths. Or almost alone ...

Locke prowled, in the manner of a bear in the moonlight, lifting up on his tiptoes, looking around, then sinking back down.

He sniffed at the air; it smelled of *Opium* by St. Laurent and *Nocturne* by Caron. To Locke it was all the same—the perfume department gave him a headache. He crept through it silently, into wristwatches. The counter ticked quietly, luminous dials glowing in the dark. His own watch was self-winding, receiving the necessary motion each day when he shook a child and flung him into the gutter.

He circled through the lower labyrinth, then ascended the frozen escalator. He entered Women's Underwear.

Satiny cups, lacy camisoles, bikini briefs in assorted colors; garter belts, girdles, half-slips with cocktail slits—Locke moved through the scantily clad dummies, hiding behind one,

25

then another, his huge meaty hand here upon a delicate wooden elbow, there on a smoothly polished thigh. The manikins stood aloof, their gestures unchanging as he groped on by them.

Ahead was Footwear—rows of toes, in every shade, pointed, wedged, and square. Locke's own shoes squeaked, as if mice inhabited them.

His peaked cap rose slowly, over the row. He gazed along the dark aisle, then dropped back down. He scuttled along the tips of the shoes, and crept into Signature Jeans, through an arch of jutting hips. He peered between a pair of feminine knees, toward a distant part of the store. Suddenly—

—an electric fireplace came on and flickering light danced in the aisle.

Locke gazed, eyes wide, then charged, shoes squeaking with fury. Skidding up to the light, he pawed the air, grasping at elusive shadows. The electric logs burned, yellow and red at his feet, but the hand that had ignited them was gone.

He switched off the fireplace with an angry snap. Darkness enclosed him again, and he stalked on.

Winifred Ingram climbed the subway stairs at 72nd Street, and stepped out into the continuing storm. It did not seem the kind that would paralyze the city and make total strangers suddenly become intimate friends in the little corner bar. It was just slush and slush wasn't intimate.

'I'm broke ...' A neighborhood vagrant swayed in front of her. '... but I'm still champ.'

'Yes,' she said, giving him a quarter so he wouldn't kill her, 'I'm sure you are.'

'I fought wit' the best.'

'So have I,' she said, recalling her husband in divorce court.

She walked on up the avenue, to 75th Street, and turned east into a row of overpriced brownstones. She slushed along to her own, wondering if she'd been robbed yet by the Christmas Junky.

She climbed the steps, put her key in the front door and pushed through, beneath a ratty wreath provided by the landlord out of some secondhand stock he'd purchased from a graveyard, one wreath for each of his dying buildings, hardening of the hot-water pipes being the principle cause of demise.

'Any mail today?' she asked the mailtable, which held envelopes for everyone but her, including people who'd left the building years before. Above the table was a big hall mirror, and in its reflection was Mrs. Winifred Ingram, hair still askew.

She leaned toward the glass, asking it dozens of questions at once, and then turning away before it could answer. It was best never to get the answer. She climbed the creaking stairs.

Footsteps above caused a momentary fumbling in her purse for the yuletide Mace—but it turned out to be just the young ballroom dance instructor from the second floor, on the way to a night of dancing with middle-aged women.

'Evening.'

'Evening ...' She always thought he might some night, on the landing, spin her around just once, but he was a very intense young gigolo, with appointments to be kept.

How nice to be kept, she thought. But would I really enjoy myself as much as I do now, with my dazzling round of subways, laundromat, and Fontaine's basement?

She put her three different keys in her assortment of locks, including an enormous iron rod wedged in the floor, and entered.

'Hel-looooooo—ohhhhhh. Are there any *bur*-glars?'

She switched on the light. Her little oasis in the night was undisturbed. She tried not to look toward the children's empty room, but found herself inevitably standing in their doorway, wishing they were there, whining, wheedling, and being their exasperating selves.

Within their room, Bobby's big glass aquarium glowed, tropical fish darting in and out of the weeds. She walked over and looked in. 'Hi, everyone, I'm home.'

She tapped ground-up flakes into the water as she'd been instructed to, and noted, with some pleasure, a striped little zebra responding.

Christmas with the fish family.

She left them to their dinner and went to the kitchen to prepare her own, something festive, with the zest of life. Baloney on toast, with wilted lettuce, yes, that's it.

'... for the woman on the move. I eat this all the time, it's quick, it frees me for other things, like working on my corns ...'

She spoke to the shadows, her nerves still jittery. With all that coffee in her, she'd spend the night staring at the ceiling.

'... Bob, darling, I love you, I've come back.' She flopped in the living room chair, put her aching feet up, and ate her baloney.

Santa Claus rode downtown to the Bowery and climbed the stairs into lightly falling snow. The bars were lit, customers falling off their stools near the steamed windows. He walked on past, hunched in his peacoat, collar up. Snowflakes clung to his cap and eyelashes, and he gave thanks that he wasn't sleeping on a bench or in a doorway. He had a little room in a crummy hotel, which was more than many of his old pals had on this night, wherever they might be—Chicago, St. Louis, or some frosty Texas town with an even colder jail.

Ahead was the mission house, men huddled inside over their stew bowls. The longest table he'd ever eaten at was in a mission house with a hundred other bums, at Christmas. That'd been quite the celebration, guys crying into their soup and talking about lost loved ones they'd dreamed up, dreams they held dear to their heart—the little wife that never was and a variety of invented sons and daughters who were now doctors, lawyers, and football players. The truth was thin soup, and everybody knew it but no one said anything, because after all, it'd been the bums' Christmas.

He crossed the street to his hotel. A pair of resident drunks were sharing a bottle on the stone steps of the crumbling establishment, as if they were homesick for concrete. But they'd be back in the hotel later on, sleeping in a bed instead of an ash can, because they'd found winter work—pushing a rack of dresses, or unloading carpets, or handing out leaflets. How long would they stay flush? Until the dice rolled over their sides, showing snake-eyes.

They greeted him, waving their bottle, and he waved back, entering the lobby. In the middle of it was a dinky tree on a table, with rusty tinsel and burned-out bulbs. As Santa Claus he felt obliged to pay his respects to it each night, by replacing a bulb or two he'd pinched from North Pole Headquarters, which had plenty to spare.

'Lookin' better all the time,' said the desk clerk from behind his wire cage, where he was safe from flying bottles, chairs, and bricks.

'It's a good little tree,' said Santa. He spruced up the limbs with a small plastic reindeer on a hook.

'How're things at the department store?'

'Kids up the gazoo.' Santa rubbed the back of his neck. 'Got me wore out.'

'Guess there must be lots of them now,' said the clerk, looking at his calendar, 'We're comin' down the stretch.'

'Worst part is when they blow their bubble gum into my beard. Makes quite a mess...' Santa peered through the wire of the cage. 'Any mail for me?' From whom? Out of what dreamed-up past, from which long-lost loved one who never was? But it never hurt to ask.

'Naw, nothin',' said the clerk, not bothering to glance

behind him. Very little mail ever arrived for the hotel's guests.

Santa said good night and walked through the pale green lobby toward the ancient elevator. The doors opened and he stepped inside, into a creaking box whose walls were cut-up with names, profane rhymes, and other inscriptions of the drifter. He took out his jacknife and scratched *S. Claus* in amongst them.

The basement door of Fontaine's Department Store was attended by an elderly nightwatchman, asleep in a padded swivel chair, hands folded on his paunch, head down, soft snores escaping his frame.

'It'd be a shame to wake him,' said Jeff Beck, and he and Sardos let themselves out, the door locking behind them, and snow falling upon them, in the street.

They circled the building, so that they might walk past their windows, where they joined the late-night spectators who were enjoying the slowly lumbering toy elephant and the dancing toy dog. The dog was wearing velvet pantaloons and twirled, paws up, a gypsy air about him. The elephant strode by him with gentle footsteps, in a bridle of silver and gold.

'Not bad,' said Sardos.

'It'll do,' said Beck.

They continued on down the block, to the central window, where the heavy red curtain hung. A few curious passers-by were trying to see through its folds, their faces pressed to the glass.

'I'm getting to like that curtain,' said Sardos.

Beck blinked bloodshot eyes, matching the color of the curtain in their hue. Then he looked at his watch. 'Everything's closed again. I'll have to do my Christmas shopping in the all-night drugstore.' He snapped up the collar on his coat. 'Do you see what you're doing to me, Dann?'

'What am I doing?'

'Forcing me to give Delfen Foam to a maiden aunt.'

'Don't exaggerate.'

'And chewable vitamins to a friend who lives for mussels in wine sauce.'

'Give them gift certificates.'

'For what—an enema bag?'

Beck stalked off into the storm, and Sardos remained on the street, gazing toward the red curtain. The window was the size of an off-Broadway stage and more spectators were coming toward it, trying to see between its folds. 'It better be good,' he heard one of them say.

A sinking feeling entered his bones, as if the marrow had been sucked out, and he walked on, to the subway, and took it downtown. A pair of professional muggers strode through the screeching car in which Sardos rode alone; ordinarily such a lone rider would have been relieved of his wallet, his watch, his ring and possibly his overcoat if it was new, but something in Sardos' concentrated air gave them the idea he carried a weird Oriental weapon which shatters kneecaps or takes out eyeballs. Actually he was dreaming of waltzing toy rabbits in a cloud-bank of fluff, but it got him off the train, untouched.

He climbed the stairs to Sheridan Square and the snow fell around him, its veil billowing in the little walks and lanes of Greenwich Village. He made his way along past the antique stores; some of the windows were well-done, and a few of them opened out into that eternity he sought, where the old dreams lived, of magic sleds and the lost palace in the clouds.

As his analyst had said, he'd raised his childhood obsession to a higher octave.

But this year his desire for perfection had turned the window into a horror show. Once, years ago, he'd gone through a similar fit over his personal wardrobe; in the space of a single evening, he put on and took off every item of clothing he owned, donning them in every possible combination, and finally ending up stark naked on the bed,

31

immobilized and chattering; in this dehumanized state of frenzy he'd been found by a friend.

Would this be the conclusion of his window? Would the curtain finally open on a naked quivering decorator sprawled out in cotton with the Three Little Pigs dancing around him?

He turned off Bleecker Street, onto Perry, and entered the front gate to his building, as a trio of mad motorcyclists roared past in a flash of chrome trim and red reflectors. They'd circle the Village all night, searching for something forgotten. 'It's unfindable,' said Sardos quietly, at the disappearing lights. But he knew that stopped no one from continuing the quest, round and round.

A heavy paneled door swung open to his key. An impeccable interior received him, staircase polished to a high gloss. He climbed the stairs to his apartment and pushed on through, to another of his mad dreams, a living space out of the Arabian Nights, with stars painted on the ceiling, arches hewn between rooms, Moorish tiles on the floors, and all of it to be scrapped when his mood changed. He'd hire Jeff to help with the heavy work and they'd redo it all again.

He dropped into the couch beneath a caliph's canopy. The place had cost him every nickel he had, and made him feel like a harem master.

Across the room, a bead curtain parted. 'You're late again.'

'Yes,' said Sardos, as he poured from a silver decanter and sank back into his white cushions.

A pale reflection moved along the squares of Moorish tile, toward the caliph's chamber. A match flickered, and the candle on the glass-topped table was lit, casting its flame in a ring upon the glass. 'You don't want supper, I suppose ...'

'No,' said Sardos.

'How about a massage?' A delicate hand gestured above the glass, firelight on its nails.

'Sure,' said Sardos, and flopped over on the couch. He stared sideways at the flame, as the hands came onto his back. He

32

groaned several times, his neck muscles relaxing. 'Did I ever tell you about the Bonwit Teller window?' He spoke toward the flame.

'No, when was that?'

'1936,' said Sardos. 'They commissioned Salvador Dali. The first thing he did was decapitate a manikin.'

The hands worked down Sardos' back. Across the room a tree of silver twinkled from floor to ceiling, its branches hung with cultured pearls. Sardos closed his eyes, and his oldest dream appeared, the first vision of his life, seen under his family's Christmas tree, the year Salvador Dali was cutting off the dummy's head. A little Sardos had crawled toward the tree, beneath which a cardboard village had been constructed, with tiny iron people on its fine gravel paths—a milkman, a mailman, a boy on skates skimming over a mirror of glass. Within each little house was a colored bulb, to light the painted windows, and the whole of it had entered his soul for life; to it he returned, to extract from this memory the secret wisdom he'd learned there.

'I hope you're not going to decapitate the reindeer,' said the voice above him.

'No,' said Sardos, 'it's been done.'

Louis Fontaine rode solmenly in the back of his limousine, reading the *Wall Street Journal*. Beside him on a swivel-tray was a cocktail and a cigar. The miniature tv was going, but the sound was off, so the image was of people jabbering and gesturing a lot of nonsense, which was Fontaine's view of people anyway.

'I'm losing money hand over fist,' he said, folding his newspaper and addressing his chauffeur through the glass partition.

'Yes sir.'

'And you are reading Dostoevski.'

The chauffeur's eyes rose to the rear view mirror, and

Fontaine leaned forward. 'What would Mr Dostoevski do in my situation?'

The chauffeur did not reply and Fontaine reached for a cigar. 'I have fallen on my office floor and beaten my fists on the carpet.'

'Yes sir.'

'It does not help sales.'

The limo moved through the snow-laden street, its headlights brightening the falling flakes. 'Sales are a matter of conditioning,' said Fontaine, leaning forward again. 'In the old days it was common for people to be executed in public. Did you know that?'

'No sir.'

Louis Fontaine had not known it either, until recently, when he'd taken down one of the gold-tooled classic novels Dann Sardos had lined his office walls with. 'There were places where you could see someone hanged or drowned in the river almost any day at all. People got a *taste* for it. They were conditioned to it.' Fontaine puffed his cigar, thoughtfully. 'Maybe I should execute someone.'

The chauffeur's gaze rose again to the rearview mirror, momentary panic crossing it. Fontaine tapped his cigar ash. 'In *that* window.' He pointed to the red-curtained center window of his own store, for they were circling the block, as Fontaine did each night, round and round, praying for his gigantic building and all its contents. 'I'll execute Dann Sardos.'

'Yes sir.'

'And his assistant. It should be quite a crowd-pleaser.'

Mad Aggie shuffled through the storm. The falling flakes seemed a curtain to her, blowing at a dark window through which she'd fallen. She stopped at a garbage can and rummaged, tossing things over her shoulder into the air, getting to the bottom, for a piece of an orange, for a blackened chestnut, for anything to keep her from starving.

34

'... Tommy ...' she called out. '... Tommy ...' The name seemed familiar, causing her to surge with feelings so strong they made her tremble. She turned in the street, to see if the mysterious Tommy was behind her, but the moon-people wove cloth behind you, blocking the view. That's why she couldn't remember anything—a rug or sheet or some kind of curtain had been woven at her back and she couldn't tear it aside no matter how hard she tried, no matter how she thrashed with her bags or butted with her head or walked backwards.

So she dragged forward, heaving a sigh, a restless one that came from the core; it told her she was still kicking, and it kept her moving.

She gnawed through the burnt chestnut and wished she was a squirrel, with a nice warm home inside a tree; squirrels knew what they were doing.

Ahead, the light of a newsdealer's stand flickered in the storm. She walked slowly up to the stand and looked through the open window. The newsdealer was heating a can of soup on a small gas burner. Magazines hung all around him and a small bulb burned over his head.

'How's business?' Aggie's cracked old voice rasped in the storm wind.

He turned slowly, heated soup can in hand, a spoon sticking out of it. He was blind, his eyes two white oysters staring at her. His hand went to the money tray, to feel if a dollar bill had landed there, but it was empty. 'You want somethin'?'

'I'm on the march,' said Aggie.

The seller spooned soup into his mouth. The street was empty of everything but the wind, turning the edges of his papers. Aggie stared at the shadows dancing around him.

'I'm crazy,' she said.

'So you can run for mayor.' The newsdealer sank his spoon back into his can and brought another steaming ration to his lips.

Aggie took another cautious step, in under his awning, out of the falling snow. She looked down at the old newspapers and empty bottles jammed in her bags; they glowed, changed color. She saw gold coins and jewels, sparkling, brilliant, bright as fire. She reached into the treasure and it melted away, hiding itself, so no one could steal from her.

'You been blind long?'

'Long enough.'

The veil of snow tucked in under the awning, a few flakes reaching the hanging bulb, touching it, vanishing.

'I know every garbage can on this block,' said Aggie.

'Yeah, well that's more than the Sanitation Department knows.' The newsdealer pointed with his spoon to a large pile of garbage bags and cans stacked against the building opposite his stand.

Aggie gave it the once-over. 'Be a couple of good meals in that,' she said, appreciatively.

The newsdealer's spoon stopped midway to his mouth. He stared sightlessly over the end of it. 'You—eat garbage?'

Aggie's head tucked down into her coat, like a turtle drawing fearfully inward. She shouldn't have spoken; panic ran through her. What if they found out, and carried all the garbage away? Or locked it inside? How could an old lady get by then?

The newsdealer held out the soup can. 'Here ...'

Aggie's arm shot up like a centerfielder's, and a second later the can was hers, on the way to her lips. 'Thanks,' she said in a hoarse croaking sigh, the noodles and little pieces of vegetable and beef tumbling down the hatch. The warmth spread through her, and she sighed again. 'I'm in Napoleon's army now ...' She drank every drop in the can, then ran her finger around inside and licked it off, after which she lowered the bone-dry can into her shopping bag. The can immediately filled with golden light, the light solidifying into gold coins, stacked to the top of the can. She brought it back out and

36

emptied the gold into the newsdealer's tray. 'Keep the change.'

His fingers skimmed the empty tray.

Aggie curtsied three times, bony old knees bowing out as she picked up the ends of her coat with two fingers, daintily. Then she looked up at the street sign, so she'd be sure to come back again for an easy touch. But the moon-force spun her around three times, before she could get a good fix on where she was. Buildings whizzed by as she spun, and then she was stumbling forward, up the avenue, the newsstand on a lost corner behind her, and the moon-weavers weaving the cloth that blinded her to all that was past.

'... Tommy ...' She resumed her chanting of the mysterious name, the name that felt like hot soup in her pot.

'... Tommy ...' Feelings were in her kneecaps and elbows and out the side of her head, and the pieces wouldn't come together.

Ahead, an all-night cafeteria showed through the storm. She walked to the front door of the place, and waited there, mad eyes watching through a wreath hung in the window. Then she entered, going quickly past the cashier while his head was down below the counter. A moment later she was on the stairs to the basement, to the rest-rooms.

She pushed through, into the ladies room, and beelined into an empty stall. She placed her shopping bags on top of the toilet where no one could steal them, and laid down, the curving base of the toilet a smooth white pillow. A toilet was one of the good sleeps you could get. She closed her eyes, and her mad dream streamed out—a dream of strangulating ether, that ether-world of dullish light where everything was one-toned, gonging.

She hugged the toilet and begged for mercy. Faces came from the strangulating gas, dullish white, grimacing at her. She saw a wreath of white swirling gas, trimmed for Christmas, and then a boy's face appeared in it, calling *Mommy* ...

The ear-splitting gong rang its one note at the center of her aching brain.

Mer-ry Christ-mas, Mom-my ...

'Who are you?' cried Aggie, into the ether-world.

I'm Tom-my, Mom-my ...

'Go away,' she groaned, for how could she ever know if it was true, or just the lying ether, taking advantage of a poor old nut.

She huddled in her coat, and squeezed her eyes shut. All those things had happened on earth, and this was the moon, the smooth white moon.

Her weariness took her, into the sigh of sleep, on the toilet floor.

God rest ye merry ...

NEXT MORNING, it was a weary Officer Locke who entered the store. Most of his night had been spent in the chase; now he walked through the aisles, size 14 shoes dragging. His first captured urchin of the day was only thrown halfway across the sidewalk and did not bounce as high as expected.

'Locke 'pears to be slippin',' said Officer Galloway Jones, monitoring the toss.

Locke stalked along, but the squeak in his shoes had lost its lively pitch, had a dull, flat sound. His usual inner vision, that of punching his way through a wall, had been diffused—there were only a few sprays of crumbling plaster in his mind's eye now, the thrust of his nature checked and weakened.

The mind of the average New Yorker is never all that stable, given the pressures brought to bear on it; at Christmas these pressures increase. On top of this, Locke was being outwitted nightly, in his own territory. As a result, his psychic equilibrium was beginning to teeter. Walking through the treasure laden aisle of the great store, he began to brood. What if he were fired? What if someone shot him? What if he shot *himself*, accidentally, with his own gun?

Absentmindedly, he whipped a teenage delinquent out a side door, and the youth managed to catch his balance instead of careening into a parked car and knotting himself around a fireplug. He whirled, thumbed his nose at Locke, and threatened to return another day.

'Locke *definitely* losin' his touch,' commented Galloway Jones at the tv screen.

Locke slipped into a back hallway, where a row of snack machines stood. He dropped a pair of quarters into the coffee dispenser and had a cup of the rotten brew; its familiar aroma, resembling boiled plastic, comforted him. He closed his eyes and napped momentarily—all security guards know how to do this—dreaming of a shadow that kept eluding him, from aisle to aisle. After ten minutes or so of this dream pursuit, Locke came awake, without so much as a twitch to show that he might have been napping.

He gazed before him, into the aisles.

'I'll find you,' he said in a low rasping voice, and turned back toward the coffee machine. He dropped in two more quarters and received a cardboard cup full of plain hot water. This he poured down the machine's drain, after which he punched the machine squarely in the face. It responded with his regular brew once more, adding a little extra sugar.

In another part of the store, where the very best coffee was being made to order, Winifred Ingram poured, chatting all the while with Mrs. Gomez. 'I'm going to be alone for Christmas,' said Winifred.

'Better alone than with a slicer like this,' said Mrs. Gomez, serving blood-flecked cheese.

'I hate being alone.'

'Well—' Mrs. Gomez paused in her slicing, '—come to my

place. I'll invite my husband's brother, the world-famous janitor.'

'I don't want to intrude.'

'On Julio you can't intrude. You'll sit, you'll talk about ash cans.'

'I hate Christmas,' said Winifred.

Mrs. Gomez cautiously resumed her slicing. 'Sure you hate Christmas. But if you were looking into Julio's beady eyes—'

'I'm afraid it wouldn't help matters much.' The spout of the coffeepot trembled. 'Though I'm sure he's very nice.'

'I wouldn't go that far.' Mrs. Gomez wiped onion-tears from her cheeks. 'But he has a nice rent-free apartment in the cellar.'

'How many rooms?'

'Six if you count the boiler; he sleeps next to it.'

'It must be warm.'

'When it's not leaking.'

They worked on, through the crowded morning, Winifred pouring, measuring, pouring again, blouse splattered with coffee stains, mind popping with caffeine overload. 'I'm getting the jitters again.'

'I need a blood transfusion,' said Mrs. Gomez, slicing on.

'Why do we do it, Lydia?' asked Winifred. 'Why are we here?'

'To buy something extra for someone we can't stand,' said Mrs. Gomez, 'in the hopes they'll improve.'

They continued until their ten-thirty break. 'Time for coffee,' said Winifred, and they marched out of the basement and up to the cafeteria. It was crowded with shoppers, but there were some empty places at the long table used by employees.

Herbert Muhlstock of Toys sat across from them, chewing unconsciously on the tip of his tie while he checked the figures on his inventory sheet. Christmas music was playing overhead, sung by a children's choir.

41

Muhlstock looked up, the tip of his tie dropping from his mouth. 'I hate that song.' He stared at the loudspeaker. 'Why do they have to play it?'

'ADDENSHUN SHOBBERS, A SPESHSHUL IS NOW GOINGDON ...'

'Why don't they put a hook up his nose?' asked Mrs. Gomez, looking at the loudspeaker.

Muhlstock returned to his inventory sheet, tie in his mouth again. Winifred gazed at him, wondering if the tip was flavored, or possibly dipped in liquid tranquilizer every morning. Upon his lapel she saw his name-tag, *Herbert Muhlstock, mgr.* Brightly, caffeine-crazed, she asked, 'What department do you manage?'

Muhlstock looked up. His eyes were compounded of rage, bewilderment at his fate, and helplessness, and resembled a pair of poached eggs, overcooked. 'Toys,' he said, slime seeming to cling to the word as it slithered from his lips.

'Well,' said Winifred, chipperly, 'that should be fun.'

Muhlstock's eyes bulged, then receded. 'Fun?'

'Yes,' said Winifred, 'with all the children—'

Muhlstock fumbled for speech, but only a few drops of spittle came. He sighed heavily, then, and looked back down at his inventory sheet. Winifred looked at Mrs. Gomez, her voice a whisper. '*Did I say something?*'

'It's the season,' said Mrs. Gomez, to which Muhlstock looked up, poached eyes swelling again.

'I have thought of a toy,' he said softly, 'which explodes when you wind it, killing everyone in the room.' He paused, and rolled his tie up his finger like a window shade, as if allowing them to see into his heart. 'I have thought of a toy that automatically short-circuits after one week and electrocutes the user. These are not normal thoughts. I've come to them only after years of *managing the toy department*!' His voice had become a shout, but no one at the table seemed to notice amidst all the other noise.

What a sensitive man, thought Winifred. She looked into his mad bulging eyes.

An intelligent face. Of course he's losing his mind but there's something here a woman can work with. Isn't there?

'... a toy,' continued Muhlstock, 'that fastens onto a finger and never lets go. That sucks children's heads inside it ...' He stood, backed away, knocking his chair over. His eyes flashed crazily up and down the table and then he strode off, gesturing wildly.

'A possibility,' said Mrs. Gomez, nodding.

'I like him,' said Winifred. 'He has a gentle manner.'

They finished their snack-break and walked back through the store to the basement. Mrs. Gomez slipped behind her counter. 'He's a little taller than Julio and he washes more often.'

'No one should be alone at Christmas,' said Winifred. 'Did you notice he wasn't wearing a wedding ring?'

'And he likes to eat ties. It's a beginning.' Mrs. Gomez resumed slicing.

The stall opened and rough hands woke Aggie from sleep. There was a policewoman above her, the woman's lips moving in the ether sound. Aggie couldn't hear, stumbled out with her bags, the policewoman following. The steps led upward to the cafeteria, and Aggie saw the morning crowd.

'... and stay out ...'

Voices suddenly popped into Aggie's ears, along with the sound of dishes and silverware, and then the revolving door spun her into the street, into another mad day.

How would she face it, she wondered? How could she possibly get through one more round of shuffling?

A dark-winged creature swooped out of the sky to greet her. *We'll find a way, Aggie,* he said, his pointed teeth flashing.

'Find breakfast,' she said, and spun three times, bags flying.

People drew away, giving her room, another nutty old lady, spinning, talking into thin air.

The bat-winged flier, the moon-guard, rose upward, up, up, up the canyon walls. Aggie lowered her bags and walked on, galoshes clicking. She had the galoshes stuffed with newspapers to keep out the cold, but one of them had begun leaking. She'd patch it with some chewing gum. She kept her eyes open for a wad, the sidewalk passing beneath her slow step, as if it were a treadmill, and music floated down from the loudspeakers in the canyon, echoing strange tongues.

'... *don we now our gay ap-par-el* ...'

She stopped at the trash basket, dug down into it.

'... *troll the an-cient Christ-mas car-ol* ...'

Like a dog burrowing for a bone, she scratched down deeper, under bottles and wrappers and empty paper cups. Breakfast appeared in the form of a soggy half-eaten danish. The sugar and cinnamon smell came to her nose and tears came to her eyes as she contemplated the bun. She popped it into her mouth, and nodded three times over the basket, marking it paid.

Ahead, a crew was pickaxing the pavement, widening an already deep hole. Aggie shuffled over.

'Tommy work here?'

One of the workers paused, leaned on his pick, lit a cigarette and raised his pick again. It came down, cracking the asphalt, scattering pieces of concrete. Aggie danced back a step, then came forward again, toward the hole. 'How far down you goin'?'

The worker half-turned, cigarette in his lips as he raised the pick again. 'How far down you want it?' The pick cracked into the pave once more.

Aggie stepped around the sawhorse barrier, and peered into the hole, at the large electric conduit below, open now, men examining its cable. She'd had one big as that plugged into her head, and it'd lifted her up into the sky. 'There's juice in that,'

44

she said, pointing her finger. The men turned, looked at her. Aggie leaned forward. 'It'll send you clear to the moon.'

One of them motioned to her. 'Get back before you fall in...'

Aggie backed slowly away. The man with the pickax removed his hard-hat and hung it on the end of the sawhorse, then raised his pick again.

Aggie gazed at the hard-hat. A dingbat flew down, large as life, and pointed to the hat. *That's for you, Aggie. They put it there for a gift so your head won't explode.*

The pickax arced through the air, hit the pave, sent concrete flying, the wielder of it wiping his brow and then repeating the swing. Aggie curtsied, put his hard-hat on over her babushka and shuffled off into the crowd, which closed around her, streams of shoppers going each way, Aggie hidden at their center. The hard-hat had a liner in it with flaps to keep her ears warm, and when she was spinning around and fell down, as she often did, the hat'd keep her from cracking her head on the pavement.

'Thanks, boys,' she said to the flying dingbats

Think nothing of it, Aggie, they said, gliding over her.

Then suddenly, words began to bubble out of Aggie's mouth, but spoken by the other woman who rode in her body: '... there used to be a guy named George, do you remember him, kind of a bald guy ...' The words floated out behind Aggie, like bubbles behind a diver in the sea. She could never understand anything this other woman said.

'... come on, Aggie, you were *married* to the poor man ...'

Her mad incantation continuing, she shuffled on, the echo of the unknown tongue following her, using her voice box, her tongue, her lips.

She looked into the gray December sky. Burning behind the blanket of mist was the star of the day. It shone between the canyons, and the winged creatures flew out of it, thumbing their noses at people.

'... and he first started noticing things, Aggie, when you

45

buried all the dishes in the backyard, and he said, Aggie, are you cracking up?'

'I don't remember none of that,' said Aggie. 'You're tellin' lies again!'

You couldn't believe anything the other woman said, Aggie knew this, for the woman had told her hundreds of lying stories, the pieces all jumbled and not fitting together.

'... took you and gave you shock treatments, you *know* you remember that ...'

Aggie nodded. She still had the electricity in her body. It still moved out of her sometimes, from her fingers and from her skull, with a terrible shivering crackle that flipped her around.

'... well, George arranged all that, Aggie. Do you remember now? Kind of a bald man with a frightened face? Remember how his eyes were like marbles he was so scared?'

People streamed past her as she struggled along with her bags, toward an unknown destination. Music continued to come from the canyon walls, walls ever angling, ever deceiving.

'... *we Three Kings of Or-ient are* ...'

Three dark demons swooped down from the canyon walls, thumbs in their ears, fingers waving, their tongues out, long and red.

'... and you were yelling, *the Russians are coming, the Russians are coming.* Don't you remember? And yanking all the shades down? You remember, Aggie, everybody remembers.'

The other woman kept working Aggie's mouth, and Aggie pointed one finger to it and shook her head, so people on the street would know it wasn't really her talking. Because what if she said something that was against the law?

She shuffled on. The dullish star of the day, burning in the ether-dream, cast a shadow on her feet. The shadow spoke to her:

'... and George died, Aggie. A building fell on him. Then you

46

were released because they let a lot of old nuts out that year. And here we are ...'

Aggie stopped at the next basket, and burrowed down into it, down through the morning papers. Her gray hair hung around her cheeks and she saw her bony old hands clawing away.

A piece of an egg sandwich surfaced.

Cluck, cluck, said the demons, drifting down, with red combs hanging over their foreheads, and claw feet curling around people's hats.

Aggie nodded three times over the basket, genuflected, and walked on.

If you left a basket unpaid, you'd find nothing in the next one.

'... George was your husband and good friend, Aggie, I'm very surprised you don't remember him. A quiet man. He worked in a deli. Too bad he don't work there now, isn't it? You could walk in and order anything in the place.'

'Lemme alone,' said Aggie, wanting to eat her egg sandwich in peace, sitting on that bench up there at the bus stop.

'Going somewhere, Aggie? Why don't you take a bus to Bellevue?'

Aggie plunked down on the bench, shopping bags between her knees, and began eating the sandwich. She felt like a pigeon, scrounging all day, but she had no wings and she couldn't levitate.

The pigeons fluttered down to the curbstone, and paraded around her, chests puffing out. Aggie threw them a corner of the bread, and studied them, wondering how they'd gotten so small, wondering how you did that, made yourself small and flew away.

She felt eyes upon her, from the other end of the bench.

People looked at you when you were crazy, but pigeons didn't care. '... here, here ...' She threw the whole sandwich to the birds. They flapped around it, pecking and cooing. The

47

woman inside Aggie said, 'Even when you were little, you'd get this faraway look in your eyes and then *nobody would know you*.'

Aggie addressed her tormentor: 'Do you know who Tommy is?'

'If I did,' said the voice, 'do you think I'd tell you?'

The lights of Headquarters twinkled brightly and the reindeers' dainty hooves moved lightly on the rooftop. Santa Claus opened the white picket fence and entered, a line of cheering children behind him. He ascended toward his throne, surreptitiously arranging his pillows, for one of them was sliding down into the seat of his voluminous pants. He tugged the pillow back up into place, where it was held by an elastic bicycle strap, two hooks clamped over his bulging foam-rubber torso.

'Ho, ho, ho ...' He turned toward the children, and they cheered him again, cheered the red suit and cap, and the great silver whiskers. 'Alright, who's first, step right up here ...'

A child, sex indeterminate, climbed onto his lap. Big limpid eyes stared up at him, full of love and trust, and a tiny hand came into his own. The magic happened then, as it did each day, his own life fading into obscurity, and only this moment existing now, in which he was Santa Claus. The child spoke, so softly Santa couldn't hear, but he put his ear close down anyway, his wig and beard enclosing the child like a cloak, in which the creature could whisper its little prayer for something seen on tv, or in dreams, or heaven knew where.

'Yes, I'll bring you that, honey,' he said, patting the little head. 'That and anything else that's in my sled.'

He pointed above him to the roof of Headquarters, where the sled waited, sparkling with sequins, ribbons, bows, as if a million little packages were inside it, enough for the whole world.

The child whispered something else, some secret from its

tiny heart, lisped and impossible to understand, but Santa nodded knowingly. He felt he did know, knew everything that was in their dreams; he stroked the child's head gently, his white glove as white as snow—and then the strange sensation came, the one he felt each day, of something lighting up inside him, as if he had a candle in his chest. The flame spread through his body and went into both his arms. He hugged the child with it, and a glow came into the child's eyes.

What am I? wondered Santa. What happens up here?

The light faded, sinking back down into him. 'Ok, my little friend, I'll see you again on Christmas Eve. Leave a plate of cookies out for me.'

The child climbed down and turned slowly, eyes still wide as it walked down faintly shining stairs, toward the picket fence where elves waited, seated on the gate. The child's form woke the electric eye and the gate swung open, two elves riding on it, as if they themselves had opened it for the child.

Behind the curtain of his unopened window, Dann Sardos gazed at the gambling dogs and skunks, their arms moving slowly back and forth as they played their cards in the village square. 'Let's put Pinocchio in the center,' said Sardos, 'as if they're playing for his body.'

'Dann, please—'

'The ultimate punishment for the enchanted boy.' Sardos spoke softly, his eyes starting to glow with inspiration. 'Sold in a game to some animals who will use him for bizarre, unnatural acts.'

Jeff Beck shook his head, and opened his tool box. 'Alright, it'll only take me ten hours of hideous work among the tiniest circuits imaginable.'

'And I know what I'm going to do with that reindeer,' said Sardos, pointing toward the beast.

'What?'

'Cut its head off.'

'Surely you jest.'

'Down to the wire frame. We'll illuminate that with pencil light and you'll see right through his head into a starry sky.'

'I can see through *your* head, into the front door of the Warren Street Employment Agency.' Beck took out his pliers, as the store loudspeaker suddenly reverberated:

'ADDENSHUN SHOBBERS, COME IN TO MEN'S UNDERWEAR—'

'—watch your language—'

'—AND TAKE 50% OFF—'

'Oh, take it all off,' said Beck, working at Pinocchio's base, removing him from his levered pedestal.

'I've got this window on the run,' said Sardos, taking a chisel to the lacquered fabric that formed the reindeer's head. 'I'm starting to understand.'

'I'm leaving tonight, Dann, at the normal hour.'

'That won't be possible.'

'I'm going to do Pinocchio for you, and fix the kangaroo's pouch and that's *it*.'

'What's wrong with the kangaroo's pouch?' Sardos turned toward the animal, who was at the opposite end of the street from Pinocchio, as if about to bounce into the village.

'You haven't noticed?' Beck switched the kangaroo on. From its pouch a little nose peeked up, lit by a red bulb. 'Wasn't he supposed to come all the way out?'

'Yes, but leave it alone. It's better this way.'

Beck knelt beside the kangaroo and shined a light into the mechanical pouch. 'The lifter on the tail is bent.' He looked up at Sardos. 'You pervert, did you do this?'

'No.'

'Who did then, the Australian Plumber's union?'

'I don't know. Somebody's in the store at night.'

'They come in here?'

'They pick the lock. You haven't noticed!'

'No.'

'Well, anyway, leave the kangaroo as it is.'

'SHOBBERS, DO YOU WAND TO LOSE WEIGHD? COME UB AND TRY BOUR EGGSERCYBLE.'

Beck clicked his pliers toward the loudspeaker. 'I'm going to come up and remove your adenoids.'

Sardos walked to the far wall, where vertical openings like the wings of a stage led to the adjacent window display. From these wings he watched the great snow-white elephant walk, its gold bridle jingling. Above it, a high-wire puppet cycled, balancing with a long pole, wheels turning, back and forth across the rope. Sardos could hear the crowd beyond the window, children calling to the toy animals, and the rest of the sidewalk audience seeming to murmur its approval and enjoyment.

'That window works.'

'So does this one,' said Beck. 'If you'd let it alone.' He lifted Pinocchio up and placed him down in the ring of card players. He looked at the floor and sighed. 'It'll only take a year off my life to rewire all this ...'

'You'll live too long anyway,' said Sardos, still watching his elephant perform.

Beck lifted a panel out of the floor, to reveal the thousand-armed frenzy of wire and levers beneath. 'Oh my god ...' He wiped a hand across his brow. '... am I really going into that again? For the hundredth time?'

'Think of it as a sacrifice to your art.'

Beck lay face down and worked his arm under the floor. 'It feels like Return of the Serpent Lady under here.'

'Everything's coded,' said Sardos.

'I threw the code away long ago.' Becker's other arm disappeared in the tangle. 'I'm working by instinct, *owwwwwch that's hot*, it must be the Bunny Sisters. While I've got their lifeline in my charred fingers, do you want anything else done with them?'

'Let them be.'

51

'Make them balance on one finger? Join them at the waist? Hang them?' Beck's head disappeared under the floor panels, and his voice was lost in the faint whirring of motors.

Louis Fontaine pressed the button to open his office door. Dann Sardos walked through.

'You're fired,' said Fontaine.

Sardos sat in a mahogany armchair, circa 1815, and helped himself to one of Fontaine's cigars. He leaned back, puffed on it gently, and gazed at the objects gracing the room—a London racing trophy, a George III writing table, a 17th century German commode. 'Louis, everything in this room has tripled in value since I found it for you.' Sardos leaned forward. 'You've got no complaint.'

'You're fired.'

Sardos flicked an ash into an art-deco ashtray, supported by nymphs. 'It's a jungle out there—' He pointed toward the street. '—you don't know what kind of nut might wind up replacing me.'

'I'll hire my nephew the hairdresser.' Fontaine leaned forward. 'Or my son the nincompoop. Or I'll do it myself. I used to fix up my own window on 101st Street and Broadway, when it was just stockings.'

'You're a long way from stockings now,' said Sardos. 'The eyes of all New York are on you.'

'Pull the curtain, Dann Sardos. Pull it today.'

'The window's not ready.'

Fontaine's eyes narrowed, his bushy eyebrows lowering. 'What's in it?'

'It's in a state of flux.'

'You're fired.'

'Louis, each year your windows are the most photographed, the ones with the longest lines—'

'This year I'm losing money. This year I want goods in the

windows—some cheese, a tin of fancy biscuits, a sport coat marked way down.'

'You're not on 101st Street anymore, Louis. You're the center of Manhattan. You're *a tradition*.'

Fontaine put his fingertips together and stared at them. His nephew the hairdresser wouldn't be any better and he might be worse; his son the nincompoop would unquestionably be worse.

'You wish to be a great artist,' said Fontaine. 'On my time.'

'Our time, Louis. You know that. I believe in my work.'

Fontaine shrugged in his custom-made jacket, sewn by his own tailors, the only ones in the store he wouldn't fire. No, and he couldn't fire Sardos either, he realized that. He couldn't fire an artist, his wife would never forgive him.

'So what are you doing in the window, day and night? You can't tell me? I *own* the window, Sardos. So tell me what you're doing.'

'I'm decapitating a reindeer.'

Fontaine gripped the edge of his desk. 'I know nothing about art, but I know what I like. And I *don't* like that.'

'It'll grow on you.'

'A headless reindeer is not Louis Fontaine's idea of Christmas.'

'I'm working toward a new definition.'

'Of what, manslaughter? Sardos, I want cotton snow and a pair of polyester slacks, reduced.'

'I'm giving you artistic ritual.'

'So did the Germans in 1938.' Fontaine leaned forward. 'I'm trying to *cheer people up*. Why? So they will buy buy buy.' He banged his gold ingot ring on the table. 'So that they will buy and be happy. To live and enjoy a store full of treasure.'

'Louis, think of yourself as a patron of the arts.' Sardos laid his hand on the arm of the chair, caressing it lightly. 'By supporting this window, you're giving something to the people which they need.'

'They need this guillotined reindeer?'

'Yes.'

Fontaine sighed, lifted his eyebrows, let them back down. 'Have I lost touch with the times? Have I lost my mind?' He seemed to be talking to himself. 'My window decorator is decapitating a reindeer for Christmas ...' He turned back to Sardos. 'You're fired.'

'Relax, Louis. Everythin's going to be alright. So you lose a few million. You've got lots more.'

Fontaine squinted from under his shaggy brows. 'People aren't buying buying buying.' He wrung his hands, adjusted his gold cufflinks. 'I've seen men like myself reduced to selling apples on a street corner.'

Sardos stood. 'I've got to get back to work.'

Fontaine watched his decorator leave, then rose himself and walked to his sliding wall panel. He opened it and looked down into the store. He raised his arms and intoned:

'Buy. Buy cheap, buy not-so-cheap, buy big.' He bowed his head toward the opening, and closed the panel.

Then he lit a cigar and walked into the executive hallway. Those executives who noticed him stiffened slightly at his approach and sought refuge in whatever lay before them on their desks.

You're fired. You're fired. You're all fired.

Myriad replacements formed in Louis Fontaine's eyes, all in the shape of his nephew the hairdresser and his nincompoop son.

He left his burning cigar in the hall tray, as a sign of his omnipotent presence, and stepped out onto the balcony above the crowd.

'Buy,' he said, raising his arms toward heaven. 'Buy the works.'

N IGHT AT FONTAINES: Officer Locke dropped to his knee and listened; something was moving in Toyland. He crept forward silently. Ahead, the darkened North Pole Headquarters slumbered, its elves in shadow, its lights extinguished.

The noise had come from in back of Santa's throne—possibly from Santa's house. Officer Locke crept forward on his hands and knees, up to the white picket fence surrounding the North Pole. He peered through the pickets, big mitts gripping a pair of them like a jailer staring into a cell. The tantalizing noise came again. The hair on the back of his head tingled with an electric charge, as if the elves sitting on the pickets above him had just blown down his neck. The electric eye triggered, the gate to the North Pole swung open and Locke crept silently through, into Santa's front yard.

Beyond him two large candy-cane pillars led to the throne. Officer Locke passed furtively between them. In another moment he was crouching by Santa's throne, from which the ho ho ho's issued forth all day but which was silent now, and dark.

Adjacent to it was a cottage with white roof and frosty windows and a large brightly-hinged door. The sound was coming from beyond the door, inside the cottage.

Locke made his move, yanking at the door, gun drawn.

'You're unner arrest!'

A shadow darted, over the window ledge and out. Locke restrained himself from emptying his revolver into Toyland and gave chase, over the picket fence and down the aisle.

His left foot met with something unstable, something rolling, a roller skate in fact, from the shelf and booby-trapping the aisle. He sailed along on it, losing balance, flailing, sinking backward, falling heavily onto the floor, the skate shooting along in front of him into darkness, where the shadow he sought had fled, blending invisibly, hidden among a thousand toys. Locke jumped to his feet and continued pursuit, out of Toyland, into the Pet Department.

Fish tanks bubbled quietly, a few tanks lit here and there, their inhabitants awake, darting to and fro, the only motion in the store; all else was stillness; neon tetras and fan-tailed guppies swam about through the swaying plants and into a painted grotto.

Locke fell down on his hands and knees, creeping beneath the row of tanks. Suddenly a fluttering sounded overhead, a cage of parakeets emptying alongside him, freed by a shadow that darted back, still holding the cage. Birds sailed by Locke, one of them excitedly dropping a souvenir on Locke's cap. Then they all flew toward the ceiling, joined by another cageful from behind Locke, where the shadow danced again.

Wingbeats came by Locke's face, golden and blue, green and yellow. Cage after cage popped open, as Locke twirled in a circle, confused by the wingbeats and swatting at birds. They chattered, squawking, then ascended higher, into the lighting fixtures overhead, and into the further reaches of the store.

★　　★　　★

Santa Claus trod wearily along Second Avenue, on the edge of the Bowery. Here and there his brethren lay heaped up in doorways, asleep, empty bottles lying in their laps. The wind whipped into these shallow caves, lifting coattails. Where a gray hand showed, it was like Santa's own—rough, leathery, joints swollen. Ankles too, were bare, and blueish toes peeked out, into the wind.

Santa felt the faint stirring of his heart's candleflame, but his touch meant nothing here. What embrace could lift a drunk from his sorrow and sleep? A man collapsed from drink is out, all the way, and traffic rolls by him. But each time Santa looked into a face in a doorway, an old face whiskered and blistered and bruised, he saw a young man who'd once run with the swiftness of youth, who'd laughed and dreamed and prayed for luck; this youthful face would then change in Santa's mind, and become still younger, become the face of a child, all innocence and joy, such as those who sat on his lap all day. The passed-out bum in the doorway ahead had been such a child somewhere, half a century ago, in some village or town—this crumpled heap of despair had been a child of the morning.

The bum was waking, was rising from his doorway, holding up a bag. '... have a drink, Johnny, have a snort on me ...' He staggered toward Santa. 'It's Chris'mas, ain't it ole buddy ...'

Santa and the drunk stood together, strangers known to each other. Santa wiped his lip. 'That's good booze.' He handed the bottle back.

'Sure, it's good booze, it's the bes' ...' The derelict whirled slowly in his tattered topcoat, waving his bottle at the buildings and toasting them all, in the bum's benediction. '... the bes' there is, Johnny ...' He pitched forward, and collapsed into a pile of plastic garbage bags, which received him like a great stuffed cushion.

Santa walked on, toward his hotel. The regulars were on the stoop, singing a Christmas carol, voices bent out-of-tune from rivers of gin they'd consumed through the years, rivers ever flowing, flowing now.

'... *oh li'l town of Bet'lehem* ... I know thish tune ... don't crowd me ...' One of them directed the other two, waving the neck of a bottle. The chorus divided, each singer singing a different song now, words and melodies colliding, equally off-key.

'Sounds like heaven, boys.' Santa walked past them, beneath a star of lightbulbs that flickered erratically over the door. He entered the pea-green interior of the hotel. The desk clerk saluted from behind his wire screen. Santa crossed the lobby to the little table tree and took an ornament from his pocket, a plastic gnome with a hook in his hat. The gnome wore Santa's colors and was bent over a pair of skis; Santa hooked him to a branch and the gnome glided on, through space.

Santa turned, back toward the clerk. 'Any mail?'

'Naw.' The clerk pointed to a leaflet on his desk. 'You see this? The neighborhood's trying to close the hotel. They say it's full of bums.'

The nearby elevator opened, and one of the hotel's guests careened out into the hall; he staggered up it, his shoulders bouncing off one wall, then the other. He struck the main lobby on the tilt, and reeled out through the front door.

'Can't think what they mean by that,' said Santa.

The desk clerk lowered his glasses and held the leaflet up, his brow furrowing. 'They want to ship the bums upstate.'

'Ever been upstate?' asked Santa. 'It's cold.'

'Well, these guys are filled with antifreeze.' The clerk nodded toward the far corner of the lobby, where two guests sat in shabby stuffed chairs, bagged bottles on the table before them. They were talking in harsh low tones, cranking out some lying tale of the trail, but the truth of their travels was strange enough. The lobby clock hummed above them, hands telling a time unrelated to that of the rest of the city, the second hand buzzing, then stopping, then starting again. Pursuing this erratic process, it circled above the bums, as if connected to their sense of the hour, which shifted in odd increments, depending on which bottle was opened.

'Yes,' said Santa, 'men get shuffled around.' He'd been shuffled himself, and when the hand was played, he usually lost.

The desk clerk shifted his eyes to a racing form on his desk, and Santa went on past the cage, toward the elevator. Its door opened. A gentleman was sleeping in it, down in the corner. Santa pressed the button for his floor and the sleeping gentleman rode up with him, as he'd been riding all night, through dreams of flight and fall.

Santa got off at his floor and walked down the hallway toward his room. Through the window at the far end of the hall, he could see the Empire State Building, shining in the dark sky. The other night he'd dreamed that he'd flown around it, in his red suit, his beard blowing wildly in the wind.

Louis Fontaine closed his office door. It was late, but of course he was still around, worrying. Today's sales had been worse than yesterday's. People were not enjoying life, and grouchy customers don't buy expensive or cheap.

'Cheer up,' he said from his balcony, as he gazed down into the darkened store.

A brightly colored bit of fluff came out of the darkness, directly toward him. He stared at it, eyes widening as it approached him through the air.

My store is haunted?

On top of everything else?

The parakeet swooped up to him, wings spreading, then banked into a dive, down and away. Fontaine leaned forward, hands gripping his balcony rail.

What kind of nonsense is this?

A moment later another bird flew by him, in the other direction, chattering to itself. Fontaine's head swiveled, as he listened to the intricate twitter, listened to it fading, far into the other reaches of the store.

Then he heard another one answering it, from an opposite corner.

Birds, thought Fontaine. Loose in the store.

He walked off his balcony, into the executive hallway, and then onto the stairs. He descended them slowly, leaving the office area and entering the aisles at Men's Wear. A suntanned male manikin stood above him, in the latest French knockoff, a sensational pair of gray slacks with a black military stripe down the seam.

Fontaine looked again. Who would buy a pair of pants like that? A marine? It's no wonder I'm losing money. I've got to fire tomorrow morning whoever bought these slacks, I probably own two dozen pairs. I could start my own West Point.

Faintly he now recollected—he himself had ordered the pants, on his wife's sayso, that these stripes were the latest thing.

But he couldn't fire his wife, as she worked at home.

'Buy, buy,' was all he could say, intoning beneath the elevated models, who stood with gloves, and canes, and gazed into the store's dark spaces. One pointed, as if toward a sight some yards off. Upon his tanned wooden finger, a parakeet suddenly perched, folding its wings around itself and staring down at Louis Fontaine.

'Get back in your cage,' said Fontaine.

He stalked on, hands behind his back, a dead cigar clenched in his teeth. Birds loose in the store. Is that a way to run a Pet Department? A buck apiece I think I paid for those parakeets, maybe more. Tomorrow if someone wants to buy one, they'll have to catch it themselves.

A twittering voice came out of the darkness toward his head. He waved it off, the bird swooping upward at the last moment, its tiny monologue still going, warbling and squawking as parakeets will.

'Buy,' said Fontaine, ignoring the bird as he continued his incantation. 'Buy hamsters, buy white mice, and ask about the special we're having on birds ...'

He circled the store, into the Pet Department, where he found the empty cages—and an embarrassed security guard.

'Locke, what are you doing here? Do you know there are parakeets flying around?'

'Yessir.'

'Well, what are you doing about it?'

Officer Locke was, at the moment, wiping lime off the brim of his cap.

Fontaine leaned forward, cigar lowering as he examined Locke's cap. Then he looked up, into the darkness, as a bird came by and gave him some lime too, on the lapel of his jacket, an Air Force decoration.

'The goods,' muttered Fontaine. 'It'll be all over Curtains, Window Shades and Rugs.'

'I'll make short work of them birds, sir,' said Officer Locke, taking out his revolver.

Fontaine placed his hand on Locke's wrist, lowering the weapon. 'No, Locke, we get $7.80 apiece for those birds. We'll have to net them first thing in the morning.'

'Yessir.'

Fontaine stared through the open doorway of the cage. 'Who opened these, Locke?'

'I don't know, sir.'

Fontaine swung a door closed. 'Some nutty old woman, I suppose. They sometimes do that sort of thing. It must have happened just before closing.'

'Yessir.'

'The Chinese say it brings good luck to free a bird.' Fontaine turned to Locke. 'It's bad luck for Bed Spreads, Linens, and

61

Towels.' He wiped the decoration from his lapel, refolded his handkerchief, and continued on through the aisle, Locke beside him. Twittering sounded on both sides of them, and then iridescent tail feathers fluttered past them, yellow and blue. 'Birds,' said Fontaine.

'Yessir,' said Locke.

They walked onto the escalator, and down its unmoving stair, into clouds of lingerie that showed faintly as the birds had shown, in delicate colors of the night.

'Let us pray.' Fontaine raised his arms overhead and began his chant, cigar held between two fingers, where it waved in the air. 'Buy, buy, buy ...'

He was answered by distant twittering.

Then, from beside them in the aisle, from a perch upon a manikin's head, came a tiny voice. *Buy ... squawk ... buy ... phreeeet.'*

Fontaine lowered his cigar, looked at Locke.

'*... buy ... phreeeet ... buy...'*

The voice receded into the depths.

'Locke,' said Fontaine,' I'm putting you in charge of this. Under no circumstances are those birds to be netted. They are to fly freely. Do you understand?'

Locke touched his lime-spattered cap brim, in a salute.

Winifred sat in the all-night automat, Muhlstock the toy manager across from her, chewing his lower lip.

'Well,' said Winifred, 'you should request a transfer out of the department.'

'I have,' said Muhlstock. 'You think I haven't? The people in Personnel are sadists.'

Winifred watched him yanking nervously at his earlobe. The poor man was not unattractive, but his face was continually stricken with a twitch that came down across his cheek to his mouth, where an unspoken word seemed to shoot sideways.

'You're in quite a state, aren't you?' she said. They were eating Jell-O. Muhlstock's kept slithering off his spoon.

'I suppose so,' said Muhlstock. The Jell-O squirted into his lap. He attempted to retrieve it and it squirted onto the floor. 'My wife left me because of all this. She couldn't bear to live with me, she said, because I had turned into a coiled spring.' He stabbed his spoon into his dish and the last of the Jell-O was sent aloft; it landed on the table and then slid slowly over the edge. Muhlstock watched it, as Christmas music came from a radio in the nearby kitchen of the automat. 'If I have to listen to one more Jingle Bells I'll kill myself.'

'It can't be that bad, can it?' asked Winifred.

'Bad?' Muhlstock's tic ran diagonally across his face, lip shooting sideways at the bottom of the run. 'The Toy Department has ruined my life.'

'Try and forget the Toy Department now,' said Winifred. 'I can tell you're the sort of man who takes his work home with him.'

'Home?' The tic ran horizontally, eyebrow rippling, as if a caterpillar were trying to crawl off Muhlstock's forehead.

'Yes. After all, it's only a job.'

'Christmas,' said Muhlstock, 'is killing me.'

'It won't last,' said Winifred.

'Neither will I.'

Winifred gave him her smile-of-compassion, the one she reserved for joggers staggering toward her on the street, their faces contorted with pain and blind determination. 'You need a hobby,' she said cheerfully.

'Darts,' said Muhlstock.

'At your local pub,' said Winifred.

'At passing children.' Muhlstock leaned forward, his crinkled tie-end lowering into his Jell-O bowl. His eyes seemed to fill with visions of his dart practice.

'Really,' said Winifred, 'you're not that kind of man. You have a kind soul.'

'Kind?' Muhlstock's lower lip ticked sideways, as if yanked by a hook.

'Yes,' said Winifred. 'A woman can see these things.'

'That's odd.' Muhlstock leaned back, his tie rising out of the Jell-O. 'My wife never saw it. She said I was a cruel, spiteful, vicious twit.'

'How unfair.'

'Oh, I don't know.' Muhlstock took the tip-end of his tie into his mouth.

He does flavor it, thought Winifred.

She spooned up the last of her own Jell-O. 'Well, I know I'm right. I can see the gentleness in a person.'

Muhlstock's tie fell from his lip. He jerked around, as if perceiving an attack from behind him. Several tables away a child was sitting down with its mother. He gazed at it suspiciously.

Winifred wondered how she could reshape the man, how he would look seated by her window in the big easy chair, with his feet up on the hassock, a chloroformed handkerchief over his face.

He turned from his nervous scrutiny of the child and began rolling his tie up his finger once more. 'When I was a boy,' he said in a low voice, 'I was perfectly behaved. Our house had a tomblike atmosphere, and every stick of furniture, every vase, every ashtray, was in its place and immaculately polished. It was such a home I foresaw for myself. But my wife—' He rolled the tie up until it was bunched like a rope at his throat. '—was a person who liked clutter. I never knew why.'

'She was probably busy with other things,' said Winifred, coming to the unknown woman's defense.

'Yes, she was in the process of serving me with divorce papers.'

'Well, that *is* time-consuming.'

'It was right before Christmas,' continued Muhlstock. 'She said she wouldn't put up with my cheap, selfish, irritable nature for one more tortured holiday. Then she took kids, car, and savings. I'm living in a furnished room.'

Winifred nodded. She'd used the same words against dearest Bob, for the stupidest reasons. Cheap, selfish, irritable. When actually he'd been dishonest, critical, and vain.

Muhlstock probed his hand with a fork, as if preparing to dine on his palm. 'I feel as if I haven't eaten all day.'

If it all went the route of his Jell-O, thought Winifred, the poor man must be starving. 'Have something on me,' she said.

'No,' he sighed, looking at his watch. 'I'm ready for the junkpile. Will you let me say goodnight?'

'Yes, of course. I'm tired too.'

They rose and walked out along the aisle of tables, their reflections going too, along a wall of mirrors. Winifred saw herself and could not believe how much she'd aged in two weeks time. Of course it's just an illusion; those pouches aren't permanently there, they're just a part of the Christmas rush, the merry madcap bustle, the parties, the champagne, the Jell-O at the automat. 'Mr Muhlstock,' she said, 'do you mind if I take your arm? I'm feeling—'

'—weak,' said Muhlstock, 'yes, so am I.' He extended it to her. 'It's these twelve-hour days. I can't offer much support—' His arm jerked in spasm. '—but you're welcome to what I have.'

Entwined, they pushed through the revolving doors.

Night had closed around Mad Aggie, the city gripped in a black gloved hand; she saw gigantic fingers clutching the tallest towers. All the shadows spoke then, you could hear them ringing from the canyon walls.

'... and heav'n and na-ture sing ...'

The dingbats came after her, swooping and diving.

We're your pals, Aggie, said the little bats.

She slipped into a stone hallway, in back of the automat,

where the garbage cans were. A yellow light shone on the cans. A rat looked up at her, nose twitching.

'Beat it,' said Aggie, waving her bags. The rat scrammed.

Aggie lifted the garbage can lid, and peeked in. The sounds of the nearby kitchen came to her, a radio playing.

'... *Fontaine's Department Store offering a fine selection of gourmet cookware ...*'

Aggie pawed through the garbage, rich tasty stuff tossed out by the eatery. The cooks and dishwashers were talking, just beyond the steamed-up window. Aggie squinted toward them. Usually guys like these gave you a break. They wouldn't run you out with a stick. They let you browse.

She, in her turn, didn't fling the garbage all around the place, but rooted neatly as she could.

Deep inside the garbage can she heard the city's cold steel ringing, and tongues crying for all manner of things.

'... *and a rich selection of coffees and teas ... fine wines and cheese, this and more—at Fontaine's Department Store ...*'

The shadows danced around her in a ring, in dingbat time, little bat-people dancing on their toes, their wings outspread. She found some eggrolls and a rubbery hamburg, and slipped them into her bag. The bags were blazing with light and treasure. Gold, she had the real thing in there. Gold she'd found in the moon-city. Aggie laughed, and ran her hand through its shining piles.

'Broke, you're broke, Aggie, who are you trying to kid?' The other woman's voice spoke in the alley, its whine dissolving Aggie's gold into mist. 'Your dough is just a dream. There's nothing in your bag but trash.'

'Shaddup,' said Aggie in a whisper. 'Don't make noise.' She nodded toward the kitchen, where a cook had glanced up, some old Chinese guy. Aggie tiptoed to the next garbage can and rifled it, her hands and head going down inside.

Metallic thunders boomed in the dark can, like a stethoscope held to the heart of the city. Aggie listened, to the deep sound of sirens and horns and crying. And the dingbat people danced toward her, holding hands, little claws extended from their membranous wings, then danced back out.

Nuts, I'm nuts, said Aggie to herself, as she glanced at them. That must be it.

She piled all the chicken wings and bones and big boiled potatoes in a piece of newspaper. Then, from out of her shopping bag, she took a smaller bag, of plastic, a special one for nights like this, for feasts.

She edged the paper-wrapped meal into the plastic bag and tucked it down inside her main bag.

She picked up the two garbage can lids, one in each hand. She stared at them.

The old Chinese cook looked up from his stove.

Aggie brought the lids together with a great *claaaaaaannnnngggg*.

The cook blinked. A dragon appeared over his head, breathing fire. The cook bent back over his stove.

Aggie placed the lids back on the garbage cans, lifted her shopping bags and walked on, to the end of the little brick alley. There she turned, nodded three times, and memorized every inch of the entry to the place, so she could find it again.

She turned, and felt the women who weave the cloth weaving it behind her, into a thick brocade through which she wouldn't be able to find the place again, ever.

That's what it is to be nuts, thought Aggie, shuffling forward onto the avenue again. That's what it is.

'There ain't no end to this,' she said to herself, and lifted her bags up higher, out of the slush.

An ambulance went by, its gray siren calling in a spiral, out into the moon-night.

'Why don't you flag it down, Aggie,' said the other woman. 'It's going to Bellevue.'

'Go take a flying jump,' said Aggie. Ahead of her was a circular park at the intersection of four paths; she'd been to this magic place before. It was by a big hotel. She hauled on toward it. The wind blew hard against her, but the flaps were down on her hard-hat. She marched on.

The bright doorways of the great hotel shone in the mouth of the night. Important moon-leaders lived there. Some were arriving now, in a big black car.

Aggie sat down on a stone bench, wind whipping around her, and watched the big shots climb out—a lady with a silver fur and a man in black.

'... could be the Queen of the Moon,' said Aggie. 'You never know.' She reached into her bag and brought out a chicken leg. She waved it toward the queen, then gnawed into it.

It was pungent, spicy. It'd warm her up alright.

I'm a queen tonight, thought Aggie, chewing on the tender meat.

Mad, said the voice inside her.

It spun a siren's wail, coming out and whirling around her.

'So, so, so,' she answered, waving her chicken bone.

The voice, fearful of chicken-magic, withdrew.

Aggie wiped her sleeve across her mouth. When she'd been Queen of England, she'd had lovely linen.

'*You* had lovely linen?' The voice came at her. 'You had nothing but rags, Aggie, because you washed everything so much it fell to pieces. Remember?'

Restless, Aggie stirred, wanting to get away. The blowing wind blew against her, singing.

... tis the season to be Aggie

Fa la-la la-la la-la la-la

Sardos tried to block the door, but Jeff Beck came at him with a hot soldering iron. 'Stand aside, Dann. I've got to shop for my aunt.'

'What did she ever do for you?' asked Sardos, desperate for Beck's help and company.

68

'She *raised me*, you selfish boor.' Beck poked with the hot tip of the iron. 'And I was an impossible child.'

'So?'

'So now I want to buy her something lovely and thoughtful.' He held up his watch. 'One or two stores are probably still open.'

'Alright,' said Sardos, standing wearily aside. 'Go ahead.'

'Thank you,' said Beck, setting down the glowing iron.

'But what do you think of the reindeer now?' Sardos pointed toward the bare wire cranium.

'Not much.'

'What could I have been thinking of? It's not turning out.'

'Things never do, remember? We live in an imperfect world. And now, Mr. Scrooge, goodnight.' Beck went through the door, closing it quickly, while Sardos was still gesturing toward his headless reindeer.

The curtained stage was now silent, except for the humming motor of the Three Little Pigs, turning in their circular dance.

A cliché, groaned Sardos. The whole window is nothing but one gigantic worn-out fairy tale.

He and Beck had given the Pigs sleazy gazes, squinty-eyed and mean, and it still wasn't working.

I could strip them naked, thought Sardos.

The sleazy-eyed Pigs winked at him, as they turned.

Pink Pigs, thought Sardos.

He stood contemplating them, his fingers nervously clicking wire-cutters.

No, it's wrong, the whole thing is wrong, it stinks from beginning to end. I've trapped myself.

He sagged into a canvas director's chair, and gazed at it all—Pigs and Wolf, dogs and skunk, Pinocchio and the kangaroo, and the Bunny Sisters. And one headless reindeer.

He flipped the main switch and everyone started moving—dogs and skunk playing cards, rabbits promenading,

Pinocchio's nose coming in and out, and the reindeer's skull-shape sinisterly glowing.

Above their little village, clouds floated, and from the clouds elves peeked in and out, riding on hidden levers. One of them held a telegram in his hand, which he was delivering down toward the village, *Arriving Soon—Santa Claus* stitched on it in winking light. Sardos wished he could reword that, but it would be expensive, and he was already over his budget.

I could change it to *Sorry I'm late.*

But it might cause premenstrual tension in certain shoppers.

Leave it as it is, it's ok.

Arriving Soon—Santa Claus.

If only I hadn't torn off the reindeer's head.

Sardos ran the palm of his hand slowly down his cheek.

Because the rest of it doesn't look too bad.

Trashy but effective.

My window is coming together.

Yet—the Bunny Sisters don't really *say* anything. What are they doing just walking along?

Sardos scratched the back of his head with the wire-cutters, then pulled at his hair a little, trying to shake out an idea. His head moved toward the Wolf, who was creeping up on the Three Little Pigs. A menu was in his back pocket, and *Roast Pork* was flashing on it.

What if I moved the Wolf, over to the Bunny Sisters?

Stand him in their path, flirtatiously.

Put the Sex Back In Christmas.

A flight of ideas broke over him and he started to work, frantically dismantling the Wolf.

Jeff will kill me for this, but I ... can't ... help ... it ...

The floor panel came up and the Wolf's inner levers showed, sliding back and forth, back and forth, squeaking quietly.

70

Sardos gazed at the intricate movements.

A cold sweat broke down his back, as he raced with his mind, over all the connections, the contacts, the sliding joints.

What lies ahead of me in there is confusion and despair. If I start like this, I'll go mad.

So I'll take some amphetamine and then start.

He went to his lunchpail and took out a diet-pill bottle, compliments of Jeff, who got them from his aunt.

Super Window Decorator Strikes.

He knelt by the Wolf and began. Above him in the clouds, an illuminated window opened and closed on levered hinges, beyond which the interior of the store could be seen, chandeliers hanging from the first floor ceiling. The window closed, opened again slowly. A parakeet flew through it, chattering. It circled the clouds and landed on an elf's head, '...phreet ... squawk ...'

Sardos looked up.

Did I hear a short circuit somewhere?

The parakeet glided down, and landed on Pinocchio's nose.

Sardos' jaw fell open. 'What an effect—'

I've got to keep that bird in here, if I have to drug it.

The bird, for its part, seemed in no hurry to leave. It flapped up to the clouds again, where it landed, then rotated its little head smoothly around and looked at Sardos with one bright eye shining.

'... buy ... phreeet ... buy ...'

Sardos approached. 'Do you want anything to eat? Seed? A cracker? Whatever you want, it's yours. Just don't leave me.'

The bird opened its yellow wings and glided down, onto the reindeer's wire head, landing on the nose.

'A bird-nosed reindeer,' said Sardos softly.

The bird's pale blue chest expanded, and it resumed chattering, tiny telegraphic sounds sputtering from it. It moved along on its little clawed feet, down the wire to the reindeer's ear, where it continued chattering, as if talking to the antlered flier, as if telling him where to turn in the great flight.

'The Air Traffic Controllers will love it.' Sardos sat down, started to sketch on his doodle pad. Aunt Betty's diet pill was kicking in and the night was young.

OFFICER LOCKE slept in Beds, framed by Rangoon rattan. His cap was over his face, but his sleep was disturbed. Birds kept fluttering through his dreams, released by a spectral figure. Locke chased the figure, through dream-aisles of merchandise. the figure always just ahead of him.

He woke in darkness to the sound of clicking billiard balls. He leapt into his shoes and crept up the aisle, from bed to bed, keeping low. Ahead was Home Recreation, lit by a lamp somewhere in the middle of it. Locke entered the department in stealth, remaining low. His path took him beneath a row of Ping-Pong tables, $179.99, with a heavy-duty steel frame against which he knocked his head. Stunned, he paused.

The sound of a pool cue being chalked came to his ears. He adjusted his cap over the lump on his forehead, and charged, out from under the Ping-Pong table, as balls clicked somewhere ahead of him.

He whipped around a card table, into the light. Directly before him was a pool table, balls rolling on its surface, cue ball kissing one into a pocket, as two others clicked in a 90-degree angle toward their pockets, into which they dropped with a soft clunk-clunk.

A pearl-inlaid cue leaned against the table, but whoever'd just used it had disappeared.

Locke stared around, still listening; the only sound was that of the two balls rolling along through the tubular return, and emerging in the ball box below.

Locke snapped off the lamp above the table. From the skylight in the roof overhead the first light of morning was showing. It was dawn in the city, with only two more shopping days until Christmas.

When the store opened, birds were flying around inside it, their bright fluttering forms swooping from perch to perch above the shoppers' heads.

'I want more birds,' said Louis Fontaine, seated at his desk, the buyer from the Pet Department seated across from him.

'Birds, Mr. Fontaine, have not been selling at all well lately.'

Fontaine's eyes narrowed. 'Didn't I recently fire you?'

'You rehired me later in the afternoon.'

'Well, get me some more birds, or I'll fire you again and afternoon will find you walking the streets.'

'Sir?'

'Birds, you idiot. Who do we get them from?'

'A breeder-importer in New Jersey.'

'Get a hundred more, to be delivered at once. When they arrive, set them loose.'

'In the store?'

'That is correct.' Fontaine pressed a button, the office door swung open and the buyer turned, toward the noise of shoppers, caroling, and announcements over the loudspeaker. He went out, into it, and the door swung inward again, leaving Fontaine in his softly lit, book-lined inner sanctum.

He pressed the intercom, connecting with his secretary. 'Get me one of the numbskulls from Publicity.'

In short time, a young man appeared. He ran the Publicity Department, was impeccably groomed, smoked continuously, and had an ulcer, given to him by the man he now faced.

'You wanted to see me?'

'Not really,' said Fontaine. 'But sit down.'

Muhlstock sat at the transformer, working the controls. A railroader's cap, one size too small, floated on his head. All around him on a large platform ran model trains, up mountain grades, through tunnels, over highway crossings. 'Woo, woo,' called Muhlstock, throwing a switch into the train yard, a long freight click-clacking in along the tracks.

'Mr. Muhlstock,' said Winifred, on her morning break, 'how charming.' She joined him near the control booth.

He uncoupled a few cars and took off again, out of the freight yard. 'It keeps me from cracking completely,' he said, looking up at her and then back down at the layout, where three trains were running simultaneously through an intricate network of track.

'Did you put all this together?'

Muhlstock nodded, twitched, threw another switch. Children were gathered around the edges of the platform, observing the progress of the trains. Muhlstock's occasional gaze, up from under his railroader's cap, was grim. He'd tried to requisition an electrified fence to put around the platform. Its denial still troubled him, but he persevered. 'Woo, woo . . .'

The trains were equipped with whistles, but Muhlstock had found that the sound, self-made, relieved him of several assorted tics. He turned back to Winifred. 'Would you like to run one?' He pointed to a transformer.

'May I?' She slipped in beside him at the controls.

'Just push it forward.' Muhlstock made room and Winifred sat down, taking hold of the throttle. In the distance, a silver passenger train responded, its coaches lit, the tiny silhouettes of its passengers showing in the windows.

'My son Bobby has trains,' she said. 'He took them with him to his father's. For the holidays. I'm sure he's having a wonderful time.' The passenger train entered a mountain tunnel, lights disappearing into its depths. 'I'll have trouble with him when he comes back, because I'm his dull everyday mother.'

'My wife has an even better arrangement,' said Muhlstock. 'I can't see my children unless there's a chaperon present. She convinced the judge I was a child molester.'

At that moment, a child reached over the edge of the platform to touch a passing caboose. 'GET BACK THERE OR I'LL KILL YOU!' Muhlstock rose from his bench and pointed a trembling finger.

'How could they ever have believed that of you, Mr. Muhlstock,' said Winifred, as her engine, a red one with white trim, came out the other side of the mountain, its headlight glowing.

'I have no idea,' said Muhlstock.

A shopper had paused in Home Furnishings, before a decorator mirror, distortion free, in a carved floral frame. 'I'll get it for Harry,' she said to the woman accompanying her on the expedition. 'He loves to look at himself.' She called to the girl behind the counter, who made a hurried sign that she'd be there in a momnt, after she finished helping the fifteen other customers who were screaming at her.

The woman stepped closer to the mirror, then saw the price. 'Never mind, it's too expensive.'

A parakeet swept down, circled once, and landed on the mirror.

'... *squawk* ... *phreet* ...' The bird walked along the frame with its little clawed feet, then twisted down and looked at itself in the glass. '... *phreeeet* ...'

The bird pecked gently at its own image, muttering what sounded like endearments.

'It's Harry to a hair,' said the woman. 'I've got to buy it.'

The trains continued round in Toyland, and nearby them Santa reigned at North Pole Headquarters, close enough to hear the click-clack-clicking of the tracks. 'Well now, little lady, and what do you want Santa Claus to bring you?'

The child breathed softly into Santa's beard, whispering her Christmas list. Her feet swung back and forth, her little bootheels knocking him on the knees; she was counting on her fingers, down the list, with grave concentration, to which Santa nodded, saying 'I see, I see.' He humphed and harumphed in his whiskers, as if thinking over the contents of his workshop. 'Yes, I think my elves can handle that. You're sure that's what you want?'

The little girl nodded quickly, gazing up at Santa, her eyes round and dark, filled with the secrets of the stars, though she wandered now in the dream of earth, the world of the stars slowly fading, soon to be lost. If I could give her anything, thought Santa, it'd just be her very own self, that plays and dances without a care. He bounced her on his bony old knee and she held one finger of his white glove, gripping it tightly with her tiny hand.

Hang on, my little friend, hang on to the secret of the stars, and all your made-up games. Don't stray so far into this crazy world of ours, that you lose the other world inside yourself, where your own stars shine.

Santa scratched in his beard, forgotten times coming faintly back to him, when he'd been a kid himself, playing outside a Mexicali canteen, and the little patch of poor earth in front of the joint had seemed like forever to him, with hills and trails you'd never finish exploring, and he never had. He closed his eyes and saw again the string of dingy bare bulbs hanging in the door of the canteen, as if it had remained lit inside him all these years; he patted the little girl's head now, and the old bulbs perked up, somebody turning a creaking generator in his

77

soul, and the glow went through his white-gloved finger to the child.

'You be good now, and I'll bring my sled right down alongside your window. Will you watch for me?'

The little girl nodded, seriously, then climbed down off his lap, very carefully, mittens hanging on a string. She looked at him one more time, and then about-faced solemnly. With small imperious steps she strode off, mittens swinging. Santa followed her with his eyes for a moment, then gazed on beyond her into Toyland, to the miniature freight yard, where the boxcars were coupling with a clacking sound. The freight pulled away then, out of the siding and onto the main track; it clicked off down the long layout, through a mountain pass and onto the distant plain far down the layout, where the tracks came together into a point. He'd traveled to that point himself, and you always found another point beyond it, where life's promise and the horizon met.

Sardos was sitting in his director's chair, staring at his toe. Aunt Betty's diet pill was wearing off, and he felt like a toasted marshmallow, with a stick through his stomach.

He looked up, at his nightmare. Crazed tinkering had led to a complete stoppage of everything in the Village of the Animals.

'. . . I don't know what you did in here,' said Jeff Beck, from under the floorboards, 'but you should be given forty years in prison for it.' A moment later he shrieked, a hot wire crisping his fingers.

'Do that again,' said Sardos, sitting up. 'The Little Pigs just jumped, kind of spastically.'

'I NEARLY ELECTROCUTED MYSELF, YOU FIG NEWTON!' Beck's head came out, fingers gripping the open floorboards. He looked toward the Pigs. 'What exactly did they do?'

'They jumped a little, then froze. Make them do it again.'

Beck went back below, his voice muffled. '... it looks like you were making *pasta* with these wires ...'

'I was crashing on your aunt's diet pills.'

'... what a fiend you are ...' Beck's exasperated voice came from further along under the floor. His tool belt creaked, and then his scream was heard again, followed by a series of muttered curses.

'That's it,' said Sardos. 'The Pigs freeze, they look around for the Wolf. Then they start dancing again. It's the final living and dramatic touch.' He swung out of his chair enthusiastically. 'Put a stop-timer on that motor, with a ten-second pause.'

'... if only I could put one on you ...' Beck lay on his back, trying to make sense of the connections hanging in his face. The floorboards creaked above him, as Sardos knelt by the Pigs.

'Jeff, put a timer on the Wolf too, so when he moves, the Pigs freeze.'

Beck sighed, took out his crimping tool. 'Ok, Dann, fine, anything you say. I've adjusted to spending the rest of my career under this floor.'

Sardos walked around the Pigs and the Wolf, then looked up into the mechanical clouds, where the parakeet was perched. 'How do you like my new treatment of the Pigs?'

'... *phreeeet ... ok Dann* ...'

Sardos held his finger up toward the tiny claws. The bird twisted its head sideways, peering down with one bright eye. 'Come on,' said Sardos. 'Let me feel those scratchy little feet.'

The bird edged slowly forward, and Sardos raised his hand as slowly, until they met, and the bird stepped onto his finger. Sardos petted the tiny white crown and stroked the little beak. 'You look just like Jeff's aunt. Don't you, yes, you are a nice little bird.' He held it up, looked it in the eye, the clever thoughtful eye of parrots.

The bird flew off his finger and perched on top of the

curtain rod, from which hung the heavy drape that blocked the window from public view. The bird turned upside down and poked its head out toward the street.

'Tell no one,' said Sardos, admonishing the tail with his finger. He sat back down in his director's chair, and stared at Animal Village. He closed his eyes and fell asleep.

The animals danced around him, the great unsolved riddle in their movements, which he sought to learn.

Mad Aggie swung along, bags rocking. The flying bat-people glided off the side of the canyon walls and descended, down through the darkness. They pulled their long ears, making faces at the evening shoppers, and then danced around Aggie. They spread their membranous wings and circled her. Aggie turned with them, waving her bags, and shoppers gave her a wide berth.

'Look at that crazy old woman,' said someone.

Aggie snapped around, but whoever said it had ducked out of sight. 'What is it, Christmas?' Aggie addressed this to the street in general, but nobody answered her. But she could tell, from all the fancy shopping bags, it was the holidays.

'Try this for a holiday,' she said, slopping along in her leaky boot, looking down at it, wondering where she'd be sleeping tonight. The toe of her boot spoke to her, the other woman's voice down there:

'You did it to yourself, Aggie. You asked for those shock treatments. With every bone in your body you said, punish me.'

'Drop dead, will you?' Aggie whipped her bags around again, and shoppers had to cut quickly away or get nailed. Aggie whirled, then straightened up, adjusted her hard-hat and pointed herself forward.

Her eyes crossed and the end of her nose appeared to her. The other woman's voice came from the tip of it, Aggie could see her sitting there, tiny and rude. '... we didn't even *have* Christmas that year, Aggie. Your poor son—'

'Don't talk about my son that way.'

'Oh, so you do remember him?'

Aggie pushed through a door, into a long echoing lobby. The walls were polished to a high gloss.

Standing inside the walls, buried deep in the reflections, was the electric shock machine. *Come here, Aggie*, said the wall.

She spun about in fear.

God, god god, please help old Aggie.

She rushed back out into the street. Great horns sounded up the avenue, from the Salvation Army band. She saw them playing in a doorway, in their black capes and hats.

She approached slowly. They had a pot hanging between them, collecting money for the moon.

Aggie reached into her bag and took out a glowing fistful of gold; it shone with brilliant light, the ancient gold of the Incas to which she was the heir. She walked over to the bell-ringer and dumped it into his pot. It landed without a sound and became invisible, so no one would steal it. The bell-ringer looked at her, looked in the empty pot, and said, 'Thank you.'

'I'm Queen of the Moon,' said Aggie.

The bell ringer adjusted the peak of his cap, and stared straight ahead, the way you're supposed to in the presence of the Queen.

Aggie raised her shopping bags and walked on. She always gave to charity. That way she'd be sure to find something in the next trash can.

The great street echoed under her. The huge abyss of the city thundered and she wondered if the atom bomb had fallen.

'... *see the bla-zing yule be-fore us* ...'

The canyons were filled with dingbats singing in the cliffs. The dark angles of the rock ledges glowed with their fires, and the whole great island of the moon-city rocked to their dancing, she could feel it beneath her feet.

'... you spoiled George's Christmas, and Tommy's. They went to pieces when you got yourself put in the hospital ...'

Aggie's elbow was talking, trying to make her feel bad, trying to make her remember. 'All that's over,' said Aggie, scuffling in the slush; she was glad the cloth had been woven behind her, so that she couldn't see or remember anymore. Feeling gnawed at her, from hurtful things she knew had happened to her but that'd been on earth and this was the moon. She was somebody else now.

A barroom door opened and some gentlemen staggered out, holding each other up. Aggie bee-lined for the door, entering under the cover of their confusion.

The lights and shadows changed. She was in, standing quietly by the door. They might not see her and she could warm up. Some kind of potted palm was standing alongside her. 'Nice place you got here,' she murmured to the tree.

Over the bar, a tv set was playing, the local news team concluding their evening report. '... there's been some *fowl* play at Fontaine's Department Store. Somebody opened the bird cages in the Pet Department and now they've got hundreds of parakeets flying around. Nobody's been able to catch them so far, and the birds seem to be enjoying themselves. So if you're going to do any last minute Christmas shopping at Fontaine's—wear your rainhat ...'

'Hey,' said Aggie, walking toward the bar, 'how about a drink?'

'How about some money,' said the bartender, staring down at her.

Aggie reached into her shopping bag and threw a handful of gold on the bar. It landed with magic silence and disappeared. The bartender looked at the empty spot. His face had big jowls and he wore dark circles under his eyes. He looked up at Aggie. He stared at her quietly for a moment, then poured her a shot. 'Make it quick.'

Aggie grabbed the shot and drank it down, the blessed warm fire going through her. She could sleep anywhere tonight, with that in her.

'Now beat it,' said the bartender.

'I'll make you a knight,' said the Queen of the Moon.

'Just make me an exit,' said the bartender, pointing toward the door.

Aggie genuflected to the bar, then turned and shuffled back out into the street. 'I'm insulated now.'

The crowd fanned out around her, giving her the usual space. She pushed some hair up under her hard-hat and shuffled forward.

'... and Tommy came to see you, Aggie, and you had your head in your hands ...' The voice spoke from inside her shopping bags.

Aggie shook them. 'Come on, get outa there.'

Her treasures and papers rattled and the voice flew away, off into the night.

But Aggie couldn't help wondering about Tommy, and who he might be. If he was her son she'd like to see him again. She could teach him how to get along, even though she was nuts. She could take him from trash can to trash can.

'... what kind of life is *that* for a child ...' The voice fluttered down from above.

Aggie looked at the street signs to figure out where she was, but no matter how long she stared at them they meant nothing to her. But there were lots of doorways alongside her, some bright, some dark. She picked one that had a radiator and went in. The radiator was cold but the hall was out of the wind.

She walked to the steps and peered up. It was some kind of crummy office building, the kind she might be able to hide in for the night.

She climbed the steps to the second floor. A single doorway shone, light coming through frosted glass. Aggie walked up to it and listened at the keyhole.

'... *lemme have about three hunnert, I wanna buy a couple extra things for the kids* ...'

'... *whatever you want, pal, but miss a payment and you'll be buyin' yourself a crutch* ...'

The voices were low, hoarse. Those kind of guys kick old ladies down stairs. Aggie tiptoed on, around the corner and up the next flight of stairs. The third floor was dark. She crept down it to the far end, and settled in. The city roared outside, but she was safe in a dark corner here.

'... *it broke your poor son's heart to see you that way, Aggie, with your head in your hands* ...'

A light came on at the end of the hall. A man was staring at her. 'You can't sleep there.'

Aggie struggled to her feet, pretended to be looking for a quarter. 'I lost some change here ...'

The man came toward her. He was wearing a velvet-collared topcoat and a gray fedora. Must be the king, thought Aggie, watching him from the corner of her eyes.

'I'm sorry,' he said quietly, as she shuffled on by him.

'Joy to the world,' said Aggie.

'I'm sorry,' he said again.

'I'm insulated,' said Aggie, and made her way back down the steps.

O FFICER LOCKE slept in a demonstration water bed, which gurgled softly beneath him as he tossed through troubled dreams, until his wrist-alarm woke him with a soft buzzing. He'd slept only an hour or so; he stared toward the ceiling, his face puffed, his mouth dry. 'I'll get him,' he said softly to himself, and swung off the rolling waters, to the floor.

The store was dark, but he knew his way, knew the twists and turns, and the many chambers. He lumbered along like the minotaur, from aisle to aisle. His tired brain produced images of hooded figures preparing to chain someone to a wall, or put them in a thumbscrew. Some comfort came to Locke through these visions, but it was incomplete, for the captive was faceless, shadowy. '... I'll get him,' repeated Locke, and the hooded components of his soul raised their dark instruments in a rallying gesture.

Then he heard it—in Sporting Goods—the *rat-tatta-tat* of a punching bag. He hurried forward through Lawn Furniture and Camping Supplies, to the edge of Sporting Goods.

Ratta-ta-ratta-ta-tat

Locke moved beneath a portable basketball goal, its net hanging just above his head; he'd played the game in his youth, was best known for crushing opposing players against the walls beyond the court. Some of his old moves started coming back to him now, in the shadow of the net. Chester Locke could still play.

He inched forward, toward the rat-tat sound. Then, crouching behind an Exercycle, he steeled himself for his best all-around move—leaping with both shoes onto the middle of someone's back.

In the shadows ahead, he could discern the outline of his quarry, fists working the bag for all it was worth, back and shoulders moving easily—but the guy's a lightweight, thought Locke, the kind I use as a canoe paddle. I've got him now.

He edged forward a little more; his prey was clad in a silver jogging suit, a style Locke recognized as one that had disappeared off a store dummy, a good expensive suit.

Locke put one knee forward, then the other; he would descend like a grand piano dropped from a window.

He was so close to the figure now, he could even make out the brand sneakers the guy wore—new from the store's shelves. Locke's own faithful footwear creaked, just once, as he sprang.

Full-force, he landed, arms wrapping around—nothing. His quarry had danced one step to the right. Locke whirled, and was struck on the nose by the punching bag; he hammered it aside and pounced again. The silver form dodged and Locke dodged with him, into a volleyball net. He thrashed, tore it to bits, leapt after the silver suit. His feet came down on a jogging machine, $1,798.76, on sale. A silver arm flew out, switched on the machine. Locke found himself running in position on a motor-driven treadmill. Speed, distance, time, and heart-rate flashed on its screen.

YOU ARE RUNNING AT 4 MILES PER HOUR

Locke leapt off, growling darkly as the shadow flashed to his

86

left, underneath the basketball goal. The figure held a new Spaulding ball in his hands, was going up for the shot. Locke tried to block it, but the ball snapped through the net and bounced off his head. The silver-suited figure laughed and Locke let loose a punch, leveling a wooden manikin, the tennis-attired sportsman cracking in two at the waist and collapsing. Locke grunted and pitched forward, arms tangling in a belt massager. A silvery arm clicked the machine on and Locke was massaged vigorously for a moment. He tore the belt in half, flung it away, and summoned all his strength for a last leap at the shadow.

He went up, and came down on an unseen trampoline, which sprung his 265-pound form into the air like a medicine ball. He floated in space momentarily, and landed on the striped roof of a safari tent. It groaned and snapped, collapsing beneath him. His fall was cushioned by the air mattress inside. He lay upon it, wrapped in canvas, and stared up into darkness.

I'll get him ... if it kills me.

He rose and scrambled forward. The taunting shadow was at the end of the aisle now, hands on its hips, as if waiting.

Locke charged. A slow-motion film would have shown his great lumbering stride creaking the floor beneath it. As it was, a camera did flash, blinding Locke. He threw up his hands, startled, and came to a skidding stop. When the round white flash had receded deeper into his brain and he could see once more, the aisle was empty.

He heard the *crrrrkk-brrzzzzzz* of a Polaroid camera ejecting a picture. He saw the camera then, setting on the end of the nearby counter. He tore the picture off and looked at its slowly forming shot—of a raging homicidal maniac, eyes bulging beneath a polished cap-brim, teeth bared, mouth contorted out of shape—Officer Locke on the job. Behind his captured form, faintly glittering, was a Christmas tree, to which a white-robed angel was attached, as if rising out of Locke's twisted cap to announce Peace On Earth.

Louis Fontaine smiled over the evening edition, spread upon the desk in his office. His birds had already been mentioned by a Broadway columnist, and Fontaine now believed that the release of the birds had been his own idea. 'I'm the only one around here who does any *thinking*.' He rose from his chair. 'I'm the only one who knows how to sell.'

It had been his hope that his son, Louis Fontaine Jr., would follow in the business, effacing all other interests and any claim to a life of his own—but his most perfect of solutions was not to be. His son, Jr., was determined to be some kind of Chinese masseur, mystically tweaking people on the toe. 'I could have taught him to sell.' Fontaine paced his office floor. 'But no, he's down in Chinatown somewhere, bending people's toes.' Fontaine turned, furious at this, but gained a measure of relief by reminding himself that he'd cut his son off without a cent.

He switched out the light in the office and stepped into the executive hallway. He walked down it slowly, trying to remember whom he'd fired today, but all store managers looked alike to Louis Fontaine—cheese-faced and smug. Well, they'd never get to the top in *his* firm. Because he held all the top positions himself.

'... bunch of pasteurized morons ...' Fontaine passed their office doors, on one of which he struck a match and lit his cigar. 'This is the greatest store in the world,' he said to himself, puffing away. 'Why? Because I run it my way.'

Smoke encircled his head in a halo. His cigar-ash remained connected as he gestured in the hall. 'Why do I run it my way instead of your way? Because—' He reinserted the cylinder into his face. '—you're morons.'

This summation seemed to give him the necessary balance to continue and he did so, strolling down the stairs, and out into the store.

'Buy, buy, buy.' He gestured with his cigar, ash still defying

gravity, tip glowing and pointing at one item after another.
'... *buy ... phreeeet ... buy ...*'

A parakeet was perched on a floor lamp, little claws gripping the rim of the shade, one eye turned toward Fontaine. '... *buy ... phreet ... buy ...*'

'You know how to sell,' said Fontaine. 'You're my kind of bird.'

The creature flew off into darkness, and Fontaine followed the pretty tail down the aisle.

'A great store like this—people come into it—they see a thousand dreams around them.' Fontaine gestured at the chandeliers in shadow, at the cases of fine watches and jewelry, all of it softly sparkling, and birds circling over it. Sure, a bird could appreciate the place—it was beautiful jungle to them, heated just right, and filled with lots of colorful perches. Sure, thought Fontaine, they like it here. They appreciate its fine atmosphere.

He gazed at the Hallway of Hanging Drapes, a lovely arrangement of goods, hung by Dann Sardos, like flags of the world—good cloth, rich, the finest and the best. 'Find better—' Fontaine poked with his cigar at the quality merchandise. '—tell me where you can find it better than this.'

'... *buy ... phreeeet ... buy ...*'

Fontaine nodded, agreeing completely, with everything he and the bird might say. 'You're my birds, and you're class birds. Like everything else I own.' His cigar-tip illuminated one hanging drape after another. He couldn't fire Sardos, not when he came up with thoughtful arrangements of goods like this. Dann Sardos understands me, even though he's crazy.

Fontaine gazed down into the first floor of the store, at the great partition that housed the front windows. 'Behind that partition Sardos is arranging his nervous breakdown. And mine, with the overtime I'm paying him for a piece of red curtain, but—'

He knows good goods, knows how to shift them around.

So I won't fire him tonight.

I'll fire him tomorrow.

Fontaine walked on, through the dark rows where his sleeping fortune rested. 'Fly, fly,' he said, waving to a pair of birds, two of the new hundred that'd been let loose. Their sly little shadows were seen everywhere now, their feathers flut-flut-fluttering. 'Adds a little life,' said Fontaine, marching along. 'Those birds are one of my best-selling marketing concepts at work. Sales rose dramatically today because of them. Could the college morons have come up with an idea like that? No. They can't think of anything but the upkeep on their condominiums. They don't have the *soul* for this store.'

Birds fluttered along over his head as he walked, arms swinging, cigar at the end of one of them. 'This marvellous palace is for the birds and Louis Fontaine.'

He saw a pair of them overhead, perched on one of his chandeliers, their iridescent tail feathers shining. 'Two mentions you've gotten in the media in one day. I'm making both of you vice-presidents. How's that?'

'... ok ... phreeeet ...'

Fontaine entered an elevator and rode it up through the store, praying as each floor was passed. He stepped out, for a special prayer service in Sporting Goods, where sales had remained slow, no one needing a $1,400 physical fitness wall unit now that they had to perform spontaneous calisthenics in their apartments in order to keep warm. But—

'Buy and be healthy. Buy and stay fit.'

A hulking shadow suddenly loomed into view, shoes squeaking.

'Locke, is that you?'

Officer Locke came forward, hat-brim twisted, owing to his flying trajectory out of a trampoline into a safari tent. 'Yessir, it's me, sir.'

'You look disheveled, Locke. Are you carrying on with the cleaning ladies?'

'No sir. You fired them.'

'Well, straighten your hat.'

Locke brought it abruptly around. Fontaine opened his coat.
'Have a cigar.'

'Thank you, sir, I could use a smoke.'

'Made by exiled Latins, Locke, working for 25 cents a day. A
better cigar you can't find in America, and the price is within
reason. In your case, it's free, but you get my point. Louis
Fontaine does not handle junk.' Fontaine gestured toward the
basketball goal. 'Look at that, for some young person to throw
a moderately priced basketball into.' Fontaine took a step
closer. 'It appears to be bent in two, Locke. What's going on in
this department?'

'I—I bumped into it, sir.'

'With what, a 24 horsepower tractor?' Fontaine leaned
forward, examining the Locke-shaped dent in the self-
standing posts. His eye was then drawn to the nearby cracked-
in-half manikin, hanging over its tennis racquet, limply
toward the floor. 'And what happened here?'

'I took a swing at it, sir. Thought it was a prowler.'

'Thought it was a prowler?' Fontaine snapped his head
around, eyebrows lifting. 'Dressed in 40% cotton shorts? This
is winter, Locke. Christmas time. Prowlers don't creep
through major department stores in athletic underwear.'

'No sir. He was—he was in a jogging suit.'

'Jogging suit? Locke, have you been drinking?'

'No sir.'

Fontaine narrowed his gaze. 'Didn't I see you working
morning and afternoon shifts today?'

'Yessir.'

'And you're working this shift too?'

'Yessir.'

'You're my kind of security guard, Locke, even though you
have ruined that goalpost.' Fontaine puffed on his cigar. 'Mark
it down 50% and affix my signature.'

Fontaine walked on, cigar in his teeth. A parakeet flew down, the flut-flut-flutter of its little wingtips touching his ear lightly, before it vanished into the darkness ahead.

Santa Claus sat in the lobby of his hotel, at a table in the corner, where a tv set was showing the evening snow. Two drunks and himself were staring at the unfocused picture. Behind the falling snow it was possible to see trembling black figures, voices consumed by static.

'... yessiree,' said one of the drunks, 'there's been nights colder'n this one, but not many ...' He lifted a bottle to his gray-whiskered face, dribbling some of its contents into his shirt but most of it into his mouth. '... for which there's just one medicine ...' He passed the bottle to Santa. '... rum from J'maica. Good fer what ails you.'

Santa slugged on the bottle, passed it to the other drunk, who was, however, engrossed in the snow. 'I seen this pit'cher before,' he said, toward the incomprehensible pattern on the tube.

'Then you got some pair of eyes,' said his companion, both gentlemen slouched in worn-out easy chairs, before a cracked glass table, on which the tv set was malfunctioning.

'... sure, it's one of them magic shows ...' said the attentive bum. 'Guy just took a chicken out of his pants leg.'

Santa leaned forward, toward an image so warped and broken into pieces a fly couldn't see it. Fuzzy white dots covered what could be a wavering human form, or the side of a house, or pretty near anything else. 'Chicken, you say?'

'... now he's doin' a card trick ...' The drunk pointed at the shivering mass before them, his own frame trembling, possibly at the same frequency. 'By golly, I seen that trick in Santa Fe, watch again how he does it ...'

The eyes of the three men remained on the set. The lobby's yellow walls were cracked in patterns as spidery as those on the tv. Outside, the winds of Manhattan howled up the avenue, whipping snow into doorways and through window cracks. The lobby was cold, the radiators dead. 'Hey,' one of the drunks called to the desk clerk, 'put some oil in the gol-durned burner.'

'Put it in yourself,' said the desk clerk from behind his screen. The owner of the building wouldn't put a teaspoon of oil in the burner if it were ten cents a barrel. The desk clerk huddled in sweater and jacket, beside his 15-watt desk lamp, on which he laid his fingers for warmth.

'... there, that's the same trick ...' The drunk shook a finger at the shuttering blur that glowed in the lobby's corner. 'That's the trick Grubby Ralph used to play on the ole Phoenix to Buffaler run—took more nickels and dimes from a poor man—' The drunk shook his head and chuckled affectionately to himself, at the thought of the card playing he'd been in.

Santa Claus gazed past the tv set, into the hall, where the Christmas Wino Carolers were propping up their conductor against a post near the door. Their voices joined in chorus once more, on the merry measure. '... *we three ... kings ... hiccup* ...' The conductor slumped forward, was caught and then restored against his post, from which he gave the downbeat, toward a standing brass spittoon. '... on key thish time, you little runt ...' He thrashed, demanding perfection, then turned back to his chorus. 'Alright, take 'er ... hiccup ... take 'er from the ... take 'er ...'

They took her, off into their own peculiar rendition, offering it to the ghosts, new and old, who inhabited the lobby.

'On top of everything else,' said Muhlstock, 'someone is hiding in the Toy Department at night.'

'How odd,' said Winifred.

'Things are getting misplaced—' Muhlstock's face twitched in its entirety, as if it were a mask some invisible hand was trying to yank off.

He and Winifred sat in a pub on Madison Avenue, a romantic little spot Winifred and her ex-husband had courted in, pretending the hamburg was steak and lingering over it, savoring each moment and gazing into each other's eyes. Muhlstock's burger arrived, and in two bites he devoured it, like a pelican swallowing a fish, as Winifred watched, amazed.

'Do you always—'

'Yes.'

'Doesn't it bother your—'

'Of course.' Muhlstock's forehead rippled like a concertina, and Winifred leaned forward, somehow expecting to hear a tune, but hearing only Muhlstock's stomach rumbling in an attempt to deal with what had just been jammed into it.

Muhlstock then poured himself a glass of beer from the frosted pitcher on the table between them. He drank it off in one gulp, foam clinging to his pencil mustache. 'This morning almost all of the toys had been shifted, after I'd straightened everything out.' He gazed at her. 'You know how I straighten everything out each night before I leave.'

'I do, I do,' said Winifred. He was, at the moment, straightening his fork and knife around his plate, lining them up, tapping them slightly, inching them forward. 'You're *extremely* conscientious,' said Winifred.

'To the point of nervous collapse.' Muhlstock began rolling his tie again, up to his throat. All of his ties, Winifred had seen, were slightly curled up at the ends, like pointed slippers. 'Who,' said Muhlstock, 'could be doing this to me?'

'Oh, it's probably just accidental,' answered Winifred cheerfully.

'Accidental?' Muhlstock's jaw snapped forward like a trap. 'I believe it's someone from Personnel. I once sent them an anonymous note.'

'Whatever for?'

'To tell them what fools they are!' cried Muhlstock. 'They're the ones who put me in Toys, instead of Accounting, where I belong. Numbers, Mrs. Ingram—'

'Please call me Winifred.'

94

'Numbers, Winifred, I could shift them, line them up, erase them, keep them all in neat little rows *forever*...' Muhlstock's pink pudgy fingers were lining up bread crumbs on the tablecloth, one to each red and white square as if in a column. 'In Accounting I could control my affliction and live like a normal human being. Recognizing this, Personnel put me in Toys, which has shattered my nerve.'

'Mr. Muhlstock—'

'Call me Herb.'

'Herb, can't you rise above it? Let the chips fall where they may?'

Muhlstock's face, in answer, underwent an up-and-down shudder as if venetian blinds were being adjusted there by a frantic chimpanzee pulling on the drawstring.

'I see,' said Winifred.

Muhlstock poured himself more beer and drank it down in his fashion, Adam's apple rippling just once as the glassful went by in a rush. 'I'm thinking of selling nuts from a wagon.'

'Won't that be terribly—cold?'

'—pushing my little nut wagon around' the city, every pistachio neatly lined up—'

Winifred knew a cherished dream when she heard one, of the kind one never follows but should. 'How nice, Herb, how very nice.' She reached out her hand, to touch his, but Muhlstock's nervous appendage flipped away and she found herself caressing his breadcrumbs. 'I've always wanted a little salvage boat,' she said, in the same dreamy tones as Muhlstock's nut wagon. 'Just a little one that went around Manhattan, from pier to pier, collecting junk.'

Muhlstock's twitching ceased momentarily, as he listened to her. 'You could arrange it all, in piles. Old tires here, scrap iron there—'

'I'm not much good at organizing,' said Winifred.

'Yes, you'd need an accountant.' Muhlstock's face continued calm, faint ripples only crossing it. Their booth was near the window of the pub, and the coldest winter to hit New York in years was blowing up the avenue, sending newspapers flying and shoppers scurrying. The wind drove against the window, but Winifred's little junk boat floated peacefully in the light of a green-shaded lamp, and Muhlstock's nut wagon crossed the tablecloth, from square to square. They ordered another pitcher of beer, and another burger for Muhlstock to ram down his throat, and grew a little tipsy about their dreams, which mingled with those of the other dreamers in the pub, to form that transparent bauble that hangs wherever people are trying to somehow get through another midnight; it's a cheap ornament and vanishes with a little *pop* at three o'clock, but while it lasts, it lasts, and that's all you can say.

Dann Sardos woke up on the floor of his window. The store was closed; a single work light burned nearby, its wire shade resting at the edge of an open floor panel. This solitary glow illuminated the Village of the Animals, its inhabitants seeming to stare through the shadows at Sardos. The slitted eyes of the Little Pigs questioned him, and the Bunny Sisters, like kin concerned with a degenerate playboy brother, urged him to get on his feet.

With considerable difficulty, he did so. The bright facades of the little village houses were all around him, gayly shuttered, quaintly trimmed, respectable animals living within them. 'If only I had another diet pill ... or some butyl nitrite to get my heart going again ...'

He groped around the village, eyelids crusted, mouth dried-up, but ideas still coming, whole new levels of design. You can't keep a window decorator down; he hangs in there until every last brain cell is burnt out.

'... *fast a-way the old year pass-es* ...' He sang to himself in a hoarse croaking voice, and continued to tinker. His idea of a bird-nosed reindeer had flowered into that of a reindeer whose entire head was birds. Casually, carefully, as if he had forever, he shaped bird figures out of pipe-stem cleaners and attached them to the frame of the deer's head.

And so, fast away the old year passed, as he worked on, scores of brilliant possibilities occurring to him. Side-by-side with these great breakthroughs came the thought that he was a fraud whose luck had only just managed to hold, until now. And now it was collapsing. Now he'd lose his job, his apartment, his friends, and his furniture.

Such grim thoughts stirred him to greater struggle with his Village of Animals; he worked like a bluster-fly, zipping from spot to spot with manic concentration, and loose wires began to appear here and there again, along with gear-wheels, levers, and springs. Once more he tore it all apart in a cold sweat. Then he picked up a can of paint remover, and considered drinking it.

Reminding himself he had a two-week vacation in Barbados coming up, he put the paint remover down, and continued his work, thinking occasionally of home, such a long time ago when he'd been a little Sardos running amuck in the backyard with a shovel, digging holes—making his first village—Frogtown, a place of mud pools and moats and little stone houses where frogs were to live. These tenants he'd found by the dozens in a nearby swamp, little ones just changed from tadpoles and no bigger than the tip of his finger. He'd brought a bottleful of them home, released them into their new dwelling, into moat and pool and stone house, and the next morning every one of them was gone.

With this memory, something seemed to turn within him.

He had an uncontrollable urge to take an ax to Animal Village, hacking it and everyone in it, to pieces. He held to the back of a chair, as this mad spiral whipped through him, a phantom image of himself gleefully destroying it all, as had other window decorators since the world began, destroying their creation, in order to be carried off and released in a padded cell.

'You're at the end of your rope,' he said to himself.

He gazed at the floor of the village, its wires hanging out like a patient whose stomach has been opened by a mad scientist.

... and no one could put Humpty Dumpty together again.

He knelt, tried to restore it somehow, before dawn, before Jeff returned. I'll connect it, forget it, and go to Barbados.

Electrical contacts blurred before him; he screwed things together that'd never been screwed together before. Fiendish laughter erupted in his throat. He flicked on the juice and the Bunny Sisters traveled crazily in their groove, crashing into the Wolf. The Wolf's timer clicked and he came on, his motor working against theirs, his nose buried in the bunnies' furry bosoms. Their mechanisms started to tremble, Bunny Sisters shaking excitedly until the Wolf's ten-second interval passed and he clicked off. The Sisters relaxed; the Wolf remained prostrate against them. Sardos nodded with satisfaction. 'Mugged for the holidays. It's New York. It's real. I like it, my psychiatrist will like it.'

He moved on to Pinocchio, who stood as before, in the midst of the card game between skunk and dogs. Sardos watched Lady Skunk's silky sensuous tail sweeping back and forth in the air.

Sardos slapped his head. 'Of course ...' He opened the floor panel and slid Pinocchio forward, closer to Lady Skunk, so that now her tail stroked the bewitched boy across the knees.

Pinocchio's nose came out.

'That's it!' cried Sardos in degenerate abandon. 'I've solved the window.'

'*Ok Dann ... phreeeeeet ...*'

His parakeet looked down at him from the clouds, then turned and flew out the little cloud-window, into the store. Sardos stood on a ladder and looked after the bird, into the depths of the store.

A silver figure stood in a far corner of the main floor, its form lit by the gently glowing *Exit* signs. It remained there for a moment, then ducked away, silvery silhouette rippling out of sight.

Sardos stepped back down, to his last tableau, Mrs. Kangaroo and her baby. 'You two are just right as you are ... understated ... subdued ...' He flipped the switch and the baby kangaroo's nose lit up, rising slowly from the pouch, the nose followed by the baby's paws, in which was fastened a Three Musketeers candy bar.

Who put this here, wondered Sardos? He devoured it hungrily, then carried the empty wrapper to the trash barrel by the door, whose lock, he saw, had been picked again, while he'd been blind and unconscious on the floor. He opened the door just a bit, and whispered a hoarse thanks into the store, to whomever it was that was sharing the long night with him.

Mad Aggie continued her web, spinning slowly through the night. The bat-people glided down from above, calling to her. Fly with us, Aggie, they said, their arms and legs becoming brightly banded as they dropped beside her, so that they glowed like candy-canes.

'I just want some sleep,' said Aggie. She'd been walking a long time, it was late. 'Don't you guys ever get tired?'

They walked along the avenue with her, their great wings folded.

Aggie ducked into a movie lobby, and marched over to a poster showing a bunch of young women in their underwear. 'Cold, girls?'

The girls smiled softly, hugging themselves.

Sure they're cold, thought Aggie. They oughta be inside with some clothes on.

She looked ahead to the door. The ticket-taker was asleep on his stool, a clump of half-torn tickets in his hand, fingers hanging loose. A bat-person swept forward and extended his wing-arm to the door. *Right through there, mother dear.*

99

Aggie hurried on by the snoozing ticket-taker, into the darkness of the theater.

'... *don't make any noise*,' whispered her big toe.

'Ok,' said Aggie, as she crept along, down the darkened aisle. A film was running; by its flickering light Aggie found an empty row and shuffled in. She took a seat at the center, a bag on each side of her, and slouched down. She looked at both her bags.

Anybody asks you, I been in here right from when the picture started.

A paying customer.

The theater was warm, dark, out of the wind, and would roll all night, she knew these kind of movies. Girls in their underwear ran all night long.

Aggie slouched down deeper in her coat, resting her tired back against the padded seat and making her magic hand signal, twisting all the fingers into a bunch of knots which she held up to the bat-boys floating overhead, knighting every one of them. Her bat-guard departed, out through the roof. Queen Aggie removed her hard-hat and tucked her head onto her shoulder; with a tired smile she closed her eyes.

Suddenly, her own crazy film was running in her head, starring a bald-headed man and a child.

It's really them, ain't it, she said to herself. That's really my husband and my little boy. That's George and that's Tommy ...

Her heart fell apart at the sight of them, and floods of anguish filled her, up and up, drowning her. Their faces were so familiar, sure, that's them, that's my family from before I went nuts. I love them and they love me.

'... *you never had a family*,' whispered a voice in her babushka. '*You made them up. They're just a dream, Aggie. They're just a film you run, night and day.*'

She stared within herself at the faces, and wondered if it was true, what the voice said, that there'd never been anybody in her life but her own crazy self.

She was too far gone in the maze to know, into that place where everything she saw was real. She was lost beyond her own recalling. Had she made up the bald head and the boy's smile?

I'm a lonely old woman, thought Aggie, burrowing deeper into her coat. I just might have.

OFFICER LOCKE walked the morning aisle, a rhinoceros hit by a tranquilizing dart; his sluggish step made him even more ominous than usual, and shoppers edged away like nervous gazelles. Security Surveillance Guard Galloway Jones followed Locke's step on his tv screen, the tiny image bright and clear, of Locke turning slowly in the middle of an aisle toward a street-kid who was handling a football.

'Uh-oh, young man,' said Jones, leaning toward the screen, 'Uncle Locke gonna heave and shake you, I'm afraid.'

Jones waited for Locke to pounce, but the football went sailing by Locke's head, to another street-kid further down the aisle. 'Them boys runnin' all kinds of plays pas' Locke today. What's goin' on, Jerome?' Jones turned to his colleague, who looked at his own screen.

'I dunno. He must be boozin' somewhere.' Jerome gestured along the bank of screens. 'Lotsa guys are boozin' today.' He in fact was one of them, having enjoyed two fingers of Christmas cheer a little earlier with the maintenance men. He was feeling good, and did not care if a football went through a window or out the door under somebody's jacket.

He glanced toward the escalator screen, picking the kids up there; they were indeed making off with the pig-skin, throwing it down the stairs, their figures descending and growing smaller until they were just a blur in the depths of the picture.

Officer Locke's own surveillance was also blurred. The little jd's hadn't been wearing silver suits, so they didn't exist. The display cabinets could get up on four legs and walk away today, but if silver didn't show, he wasn't interested.

I'll get him, thought Locke, tonight.

Locke moved numbly forward. He was beat, sure; he hadn't slept much. But he could feel the pattern falling into place. Tonight he'd drop out of the sky on top of the bozo in the silver suit, tonight he'd know where to be.

He entered the Drapery Department, his step growing softer there, muffled by the carpets and the heavy hanging fabric.

Tonight, he thought, I'll nail him.

But I've got to get forty winks first or I'll never make it.

He'd done a lot of floorwalking in his day but he'd pushed himself over the limit on this one. Therefore he stepped into one of his favorite resting places, behind a pair of insulated drapes, the material so thick and pleated that his form did not show through it—except for the peak of his hat, which he took off and set on the floor, beside his massive shoes. These too were covered by the luxurious drape.

Here a security guard could take a little nap, standing up.

Locke leaned back against the wall of the department, and let his head go down. In three seconds he was asleep, into the dreaming mind of the store—bells ringing, voices calling, shoppers rumbling, everyone talking, with a humming that took him ever deeper into unconsciousness.

Have you ever slept standing up in a store? It's a trance-like state, whose sensation Locke knew well, having napped in this way for a great number of years. His swaying form behind the drape actually moved very little, so that a passing shopper might think that it was just the ventilator blowing behind the curtain, when actually it was Locke snoring.

His face had collapsed into jowly slumber, lips flubbering softly, as he regained his precious energies. In his dream he chased a mercurial figure, who slipped through his hands again and again, leaving only a silvery phosphorescence on his fingertips.

A parakeet flew to the top of the drape, perching on the rod, beneath which Locke slumbered.

'... *phreet ... friiiickkk ... qriiccckkk ... phreeet ...*' The bird was beaking itself under the wing, attending to the alignment of some feather or other, but one eye still looked out at the passing shoppers. They, in their turn, stopped before it.

Locke slept beyond their gaze, enfolded in 71% cotton.

The material was embroidered with flowers sewn in exotic colors. Locke's heavy breathing made this field of blossoms move in a gentle breeze.

'... *Locke* ...' crackled the bird, as if recalling conversation from the night before, in a voice reminiscent of Louis Fontaine. '... *phreeeet ... friiiccckk ...*'

Locke did not respond, the bird's voice just a piece of crackling static on the surface of his mind, while he was much deeper, swathed in cotton slumber.

The bird flew off. The shoppers walked away. Locke slept on.

When he awoke sometime later, the first thing he did was reach down and put on his security cap. Something dropped from inside it onto his head, rolling around there. He removed the cap and found a Milky Way candy bar.

His eyes shot along the shadows behind the drapes and he reached out, groping for the intruder who'd slipped in on him, but whoever it was had gone, as quietly as they'd come.

Locke contemplated the candy bar. It was, he decided, evidence.

It was also a candy bar. Few can have such a thing in their possession for long without falling slave to it. Locke was not one of these people. He ate the evidence.

Thus, nourished and rested he came out from behind the drapes.

Sales were up again today. Louis Fontaine could feel it, as he opened his Chippendale cigar stand. A feeling came through the office wall, that the store had been switched *on*. His birds had done it.

'They cheer people up,' he said, and cheered up himself, at the thought of firing somebody.

He gazed around his office, lost in thought, hands behind his back. 'Those birds are just another example of my natural salesmanship at work.'

In prideful reflection, he paced slowly back and forth on his thick carpet, trying to remember exactly how the idea of letting the birds loose had come to him. Then he remembered that some nutty old lady had let the birds loose.

Nutty old ladies did things like that in a store. If one of them was doing anything like that at the moment, he hoped they were being thrown out. But he was grateful to the one who'd let the birds loose.

'A nutty old lady,' said Fontaine to himself, 'came up with a better idea than anybody in Advertising and Publicity ever did.'

He exited his office and strode down the hall to Advertising and Publicity, where he looked in and fired everyone. Having relieved excess tension in this manner, he approached the executive staircase.

The rumble of the store grew louder until presently he was out on the floor himself. He roamed, interfering in various departments, confusing the issue for his flustered clerks, who were already seeing double.

'ADDENSHUN SHOBBERS, A SURPRIBE CHRISTMAS DISCOUND ID NOW BEING GIBBEN DIN HOME BURNISHINGS.'

'That man has to be fired at once,' said Fontaine, coming out from behind a counter, only to recall the man was his brother-in-law. What does he have up his nose, a ham sandwich?

Trying to ignore the voice of his brother-in-law, Fontaine walked on, down through the store, until he came to the locked door leading to the front window display. He banged on it. 'Dann Sardos! This is Louis Fontaine! You're fired! Do you hear me?'

'*Ok, Louis* ...' Sardos's muffled voice came from beyond the partition, but the door remained closed. Fontaine listened to the sound of a hammer, and then the hum of a motor.

The mechanical window opened, and a parakeet flew out. '... *ok Louis ... phreeeeet* ...'

Fontaine swung after the bird. 'What's he up to in there?'

The fluttering blue and gold tail traveled on, disappearing into the massive chandelier that graced the center of the first floor ceiling. Fontaine walked under it and looked up. It was filled with birds, their little claws clinging to the chandelier as to a great hanging vine of light, with crystalline leaves and fruit.

Fontaine raised his arms, gesturing with an unlit cigar. 'Let me hear it ...'

'... *buy ... phreeet ... buy* ...'

'You're good birds.' He stuck the cigar back in his face, and walked on.

Santa Claus ate his lunch in the basement, in his dressing room, leaning back against a manikin from whose slender wooden hand his whiskers dangled, by their elastic band. He finished a sandwich, and lit a butt. Overhead, the store continued its ceaseless rumbling, but the basement was quiet. He smoked, leaning forward, elbows on his knees, eyes on the floor. Old scenes came and went—lumber camps, tomato farms, bread lines and blueberry fields—a lot of bits and pieces sewn into ragged memory. He continued staring, at his hands. One of them was gloved in a cloth white as snow. The other was stained brown at the fingertips, and shook when he raised the butt.

He was pretty well shot. Too much booze, he guessed, and the cold had gotten into his kidneys somewheres and never really left; next Christmas would find him down, maybe way down, maybe underneath the blueberries.

He ground the cigarette under his bootheel and lifted his beard from the manikin's long finger. He slipped the elastic band around his head and adjusted the whiskers under his nose.

Half-suffocate a man, a beard like this.

He arranged his pillows, cap and gloves, and left the storeroom. Usually he had a little snort of rum after lunch, to carry him through the afternoon, but he'd forgotten to bring the old medicine bottle from home today, and his ho-ho-ho wasn't going to be quite as merry.

He went up the steps and entered the store. Shoppers smiled at him, and waved, and he waved back, through the aisles to the escalator. He rode up to the next floor. Here too, shoppers greeted him, calling hello, and he wished them a merry Christmas. His face was completely hidden except for nose and eyes, and his pillows gave him the feeling of moving along inside a kind of fortress. Nobody could know who he was; he was Santa Claus, that's all, and anyone who looked his way saw it that way—saw old Father Christmas. Their smiles and their hellos were to that old-timer and it was that old-timer who answered them.

'... Merry Christmas ... Merry Christmas ...'

'ADDENSHUN, BOYS AND GIRLS, I'M TOLD THAT SANTA CLAUBS ID ON HID BAY BACK TO TOYLAMB. WHY DON'T YOU HURR-BEE ON UBB THERE AND

By the time he reached the next escalator, the kiddos had spotted him and were dragging their mothers along in his wake.

Too bad he'd forgotten the medicine bottle, it was going to be a crowded afternoon.

Maybe the maintenance boys would be by later, and he could duck into North Pole Headquarters with them. Just a quick one, just a small nip, that's all he needed, a mere taste of the old mule.

'... Merry Christmas ... Merry Christmas ...'

He came off the escalator, hands folded on his great stomach, which preceded him, queen-sized. The girls in Gift Wrapping waved to him from their tangle of ribbon and bows; some of them had bows pinned in their hair or tied around their wrists; their hands flew, snapping boxes open, arranging tissue and gift, and closing the whole thing up again with paper and ribbon, all of it less time than it'd take him to roll a smoke of Bull Durham.

'... Merry Christmas ...' His tongue was hanging out now alright, and a couple dozen kids were following him, and a hundred more would be waiting above.

A sip of redeye, just one, Lord. Not so's I'm blind in my beard, but so's I can do the show. I know you'll provide.

He got on the last escalator flight, riding backward, waving to the children who were following like a herd of little mountain goats, up to the top. They'd stick their lollipops in his whiskers, dribble on his suit, step on his bunions; it'd be a long afternoon. '... right this way, boys and girls, you just follow Santa ...' He waved, riding backward off the escalator, into Toyland, and they followed, in a shoving, whining, screaming, sobbing, screeching-with-laughter line, toward North Pole Headquarters.

The electric eye gate in the picket fence swung magically open, and he entered his snowy front yard. Upon the roof of his workshop the dainty reindeer danced, legs rising and falling slowly, as if they were taking a running start, off into the sky with the twinkling sled.

He took down the Out To Lunch sign that hung on the tasseled cord across his throne. Then, as he was about to sit down he saw, nestled in the big red cushion, a box of candy Santas.

'Well now, boys and girls, just a moment here while I have dessert ...'

He sat on his throne, and examined the candy. It was the best the store had, he saw, imported from Holland. He unwrapped one and popped the chocolate Santa through his whiskers. It opened on his tongue, filled with rum.

He swallowed, and lifted his eyes to Headquarters.

Much obliged.

Mad Aggie was shown out of the porno theater at dawn, shopping bags swinging. The morning light struck her eyes, and she came out fearfully, looking up and down the street. Which way should an old dingbat go?

At the end of the street, police cars had their lights on.

So Aggie will go the other way.

Good morning, Aggie, said the little bat-people, holding each other's little hands and dancing around Aggie.

Just follow the dingbats, thought Aggie. Those bats always know where an old lady can get some help.

She smelled a hamburger joint up ahead. There was a good-looking garbage pile outside the place. 'Things are pickin' up,' said Aggie, waving to a man on his way to work, briefcase in hand.

He looked at her, momentarily.

'Lots more garbage on this street this year,' said Aggie, pointing to the piled cans and bags.

The man looked. 'There certainly is.' He adjusted his coat lapels and walked on.

The Mayor of the Moon, thought Aggie, watching the gentleman as he continued down the street. Then she turned, back to the garbage pile, and carefully tore open a bag.

Lots of good stuff here, look at these eggshells, got some egg still hanging around inside them.

Aggie slurped the raw egg down.

'Can't beat that.' She held the half-shell up like a cup, to the sun of the moon. The dingbat fliers swooped down and circled her speckled cup.

We thought you'd like it, Aggie, they said, and flew in toward her, little claw feet out, big nails pointing, and then they danced away, twisting and showing their horned back toes.

Above the piled bags, in the steamed window, was a Greek kid chopping onions. He looked at Aggie as he chopped.

Aggie went to the best-looking bag in the pile, burying herself in its green plastic plushness. '... just an old crackpot from somewhere, lookin' for a bite to eat, don't pay any attention ...'

Aggie dug, finding a nest of home-fried potatoes. And what's this over here?

A pile of brain cells.

Guess they must have operated and threw it away.

She picked up the human brain and put it in her shopping bag, beside the rest of her treasure. Gray mist rose from it, swirling and blowing.

The cook looked up again, his eyes heavy with morning. He pointed a thumb at the coffee urn, and glanced back at Aggie.

'Right here, sonny.' Aggie hopped toward the door, opened it and went inside. She walked to the end of the counter, where the cook was setting out the steaming cup of java for her.

She looked up and down the counter. The restaurant was empty.

She put the cup to her lips. The hot black liquid went down her throat.

'You want sugar?' The kid slid it over.

'That's the stuff.' Aggie turned it upside down and poured out a measure for herself, and one for the lady who rode around inside her.

The cook put cream down, went back to his counter, and resumed chopping. Aggie poured out the cream, good thick stuff for the bones. She stirred it in and drank the coffee down. 'Where is everybody?'

'... place is dead ...' The cook chopped onions into his frying pan, stirred them around. '... here, lemme give you an egg on a bun, then you got to beat it ...'

'Right, right.' Aggie turned on her stool, and took out a cigarette butt. She lit up the stubbly end, and smoked while the kid cooked up the egg.

'... and throw in some of this brain ...' Aggie reached into her bag and tossed a handful toward the griddle.

It floated, slow and gray through the air. She watched it glide down, crackling, into the cook's pan.

The restaurant was warm, she could feel the heat collecting in her overcoat, down into all the wads of padded newspaper she insulated with

The kid stirred the scrambled egg, then turned it out onto a bun. 'Here you go.'

'You're a nice boy. You're good to your mother.'

The cook bent under the counter for something, and Aggie bent too, into her shopping bags. She put the sandwich in, and took a gold coin out. She laid it on the counter, where it began to fade, slowly, into the wood. 'Keep this for yourself.'

The cook came back up, looked at the empty counter. '... yeah, thanks ...'

Aggie walked out of the restaurant, into the street. It was cold but she had coffee inside her now, and it'd make a hot water bottle out of her stomach for about two hours.

She whirled in the street, three times, her bags in the air. The canyon walls whizzed around her as she turned, and all the dingbats went turning the other way, flapping their wings slowly, round and round her head.

She spun to a stop in the slush, nose pointed. She could smell the fish market at the other side of the island.

She could spend a year or so getting there, at the rate she walked. Be there by next Christmas.

She swung on, head raised toward the canyon heights, up the iron walls to the top where the dark angels flew. They were flying in rings around the towers. And there was George's great bald head in the sky.

'George, is it really you I'm always seein'?'

No, Aggie, you are seeing a lot of different things, all of them discombobulated.

Aggie paused over a dark subterranean mouth. It rumbled, and a bunch of bats came up out of it, fangs dripping.

Aggie stared down the steps. On the subway landing, huddled in the corner, was an old wino. Aggie hoisted her bags and descended the stairs. 'Hey ...' She shook him by the shoulder.

He looked up at her. She leaned toward him.

'Is your name George?'

The drunk blinked slowly, eyes glazed. '... dunno ... lemme ... lemme think ...'

'How would you like a bottle of Jack Daniel's,' said Aggie, and rooted in her shopping bag. She hauled out a big shining bottle and handed it to the drunk.

He shook it. '... empty ...'

'Unscrew that lid,' said Aggie, pointing her gnarled finger.

The drunk worked his thumb slowly on the cap. He held the mouth of the bottle up to his eye. '... empty as she can get ...' He lobbed the bottle down the steps.

'You sure your name ain't George? I'm looking for a man named George.'

'What for?' The wino was pushing himself up off the landing, fingernails scraping along the wall as he struggled with its surface. He straightened, swayed, ran his hand through his hair.

'He was my husband,' said Aggie.

'... he's long gone ...' The drunk grabbed the stair-rail and hauled himself up the steps.

Aggie followed him, back up into the light. The drunk was digging in his pockets for things that weren't there, stumbling forward, on his way.

Aggie's eyes crossed, and the sidewalk doubled. She banged on her hard-hat, and her eyes straightened again, but George had vanished, into the crowd.

'Be good,' said Aggie to his vanished form. 'Take care of Tommy.'

'... you ruined your boy's life, Aggie,' said the woman's voice. 'Of that you can be sure.'

'He's got a good job,' said Aggie. 'He's cookin' in a joint back there somewhere.' She ran a thumb over her shoulder. Passing shoppers glanced at her dialogue, faces curious for a moment, then blinking and passing.

Just another old nut, whispered the dingbats, but she's mother to us. They thumbed their noses at the people who stepped away from Aggie's stumbling sawed-off figure.

She shuffled forward, chin out, toothless face set for a determined march. She was going somewhere, somewhere ahead.

The wind drove against her, but this was the direction she was supposed to go. Whenever she'd whirled three times and pointed, that was it, that was the direction.

She could feel the magnet in the maze, the great big one somewhere at the center. When she found the big magnet of the moon, she'd be ok. All the cracked thoughts would be drawn out of her head, like hairpins. And she'd be wonderful and not crazy anymore.

She hurried along, wanting to get there soon. From the canyon walls came the dingbat chorus.

'... *six geese a-laying, seven swans a-swimming* ...'

I should have a camel, thought Aggie, and by lunatic magic it was there between her bowed old legs. She sighed and settled around its hump, the tired feeling gone from her knees.

'I'm Queen of the Moon!' shouted Aggie, patting her shopping bags. The passing stream of shoppers widened around her, bellying out, giving her the maniac's breadth.

Aggie felt a pin fly out of her hair. She must be getting close to the moon-magnet. Another year or two of walking might get her there.

Or it could be just around the corner. You never knew. She'd walked this maze for many millions of years, and it always had a surprise for you. '... I know this town, Tommy, and I'll teach you how to get around ...'

The wind whipped a newspaper along the street. Aggie saw it was one of the magic papers, becoming a great bird flapping. A bird like that would lead her straight to the magnet. She jumped into the street after it, to catch its tail.

A horn sounded loudly behind her, and she jumped back, losing her balance. The buildings whirled and she up-ended.

Oh god, I'm going down.

She landed, bags flying. Her morning egg sandwhich on a bun sailed out of her bag and hit the street. The honking car ran over it. Aggie, seated in the slush, watched the car roll by, long as a railroad coach and black as the wings of a bat. Behind its tinted windows she saw a king, talking to another king. Moon kings, a pair of them.

Their back wheels were finishing what the front wheels started, flattening her sandwich.

'Big shots!' Aggie waved her fist. 'Think you own the moon.' She pulled herself out of the slush and crouched over her sandwich, then scraped it up, muck and snow embedded in it. '... flat as a taco ...'

She stuffed it in her bag, and watched the kings' car disappearing down the block, as they drove toward their

114

palace, with part of her sandwich on their tire.

I'll get them, said George, from above. They can't run over my old lady's sandwich and get away with it.

'... forget it, don't get yourself worked up ...' Aggie waved him off, wiping the slush from her overcoat and cheeks. 'I'm wet but I'm insulated.' She patted her paper-crinkling hips. She'd be dry by next month. She'd dry out for springtime.

Muhlstock stood by Winifred's coffee counter, the contents of his cup splashing about in his nervous grip. He stared at its troubled surface, as if expecting a toy submarine to surface there, with a torpedo aimed at himself. Finding none emerging and satisfied it was only a local storm, he swallowed the contents, as was his custom, in one gulp. 'Thank you,' he said, setting the cup down on Winifred's counter with a bang; its plastic handle cracked off in his fingers. He put the handle in his pocket.

'How are you feeling?' asked Winifred, her face screwed into its day-long smile which about three o'clock made her ears start to ache.

'I'm just dandy,' said Muhlstock, face twitching as if army ants were biting it in several dozen places.

'Well, then,' chimed in Mrs. Gomez, whose fingers were now bandaged to the second knuckle, 'we'll probably make it till closing time.'

She sliced him a piece of cheese and Muhlstock made short work of the morsel. 'We should have a party,' he said, blinking some twenty times in rapid succession, followed by one succinct rightward snap of the head, which ended the ocular spasm. 'After all, it's Christmas Eve.'

'Love to,' said Winifred.

'In the Toy Department,' said Muhlstock. 'Just before the store closes.'

'... *cheese, ladies* ...' Mrs. Gomez was turning toward the customers and raising and lowering the blade of her slicer. '...

have some of ... ow Santa Maria ... this lovely cheese ...'

Muhlstock leaned against Winifred's side of the counter, and said, nearly in a whisper, 'I got your candy bar.'

Winifred looked at him, her-day-long smile altering slightly, a muted question playing over it. Muhlstock rocked up and down while waving his elbows. She kept looking for a switch somewhere, to click him off. His elbows came to his sides with a clapping sound.

'Very clever of you, putting it in my engineer's cap.' He began a little light parachuting, lifting his coattails with two fingers. 'Kind of you. Yes, thank you.' He seemed to land lightly, knees buckling slightly. 'It added a single moment of—of relatedness—to my day.'

'Mr. Muhlstock—Herb—may I offer you more coffee?' Winifred raised her pot, pouring for him, and for some other customers moving in beside him. *'All the acid has been removed by the action of the Miracle Filter ...'*

'You're very good at this,' said Muhlstock, lifting his cup and sniffing the brew, as Winifred made the rounds of the cups, along the counter to the waiting shoppers, for whom some brew was everything at this moment, with ten more presents left to buy and only tonight left in which to find them. *'... drink up ... you'll find it's delicious ... it's the Miracle Filter ...* hello, Mr. Muhlstock, did you finish yours already ... in one fast gulp ... let me give you another ...'

'Thank you, no, that's enough,' said Muhlstock. 'I—I have a tendency toward bouncing—' He went up, down, up. '—and I mustn't exaggerate it.'

He continued popping around in place, his gaze moving nervously over the crowd. 'I suppose I should be getting back—'

'Oh relax,' said Winifred. 'What does it matter now, the day's almost over.'

'Ragamuffins,' said Muhlstock in a crisp military salute. 'I must deal with them.' He straightened his shoulders several

116

times, like a New York pigeon considering takeoff.

His flight attracted other fliers, a parakeet sweeping down past him. '... *phreeeet ... criiickk ... phreeet ...*'

'Here, birdie,' said Mrs. Gomez, who'd been trying for days to get them to eat cheese, but they may have feared her slicer for they never got closer than the awning of the counter, on which one of them now perched, looking down at Muhlstock.

'It's the smartest thing *this* store has ever done,' said Muhlstock. 'I'm sure the idea didn't originate with Personnel.'

The bird walked along the edge of the awning, claws holding to the brass rod. It turned slowly, and hung upside down, gazing at Winifred. '... *phreeeet ... griiicckk ... phreeeeet ...*'

Winifred paused in her pouring to gaze back at the bird's soft blue breast with its lovely white collar. The delicate wing feathers shone brightly, like tropic flowers, and she wanted to touch it, to pet the tiny head with her fingertip. 'How sweet you are ... come and talk to me ...'

The bird might have, had not Muhlstock's own finger gone off with a snap, exploding upward like the barrel of a gun. 'Oh, I'm sorry—'

The bird flew away, over the heads of the shoppers, one of whom quickly felt the back of his head, then looked into his hand, at a 20% discount.

'I really must be going,' said Muhlstock, teetering toward Winifred's counter. 'My breakdown—excuse me, my *break*—is over now.' He looked at his watch, wound it compulsively, as he did each hour, listening to the tightening spring until, like himself, it was just on the point of snapping. Then he looked at Winifred and turned about face.

Then, turning back again: 'Just before closing time. Come up ...' He pointed to the ceiling.

Winifred nodded, pouring on down the counter, from customer to customer. 'I'll be there.'

Muhlstock popped on his toes. While in this ballet position his hands flew into his pocket, then out. 'Thanks again for the

117

candy bar.' He shredded the wrapper in his pocket. Following this he inserted the candy bar itself into his mouth. Again, like the pelican, his neck worked, just once, and the bar was gone.

I must never give him anything bigger than an Almond Joy, thought Winifred.

Yet another part of her thought it would be interesting to see Herbert Muhlstock eat an entire baked potato. Or a pot pie. Or anything, really. She was, she realized, getting used to him.

He departed, into the aisle, and through the steam from her spout she followed his progress, his head popping up and down as he made his way through the crowd.

'He's buoyant,' said Mrs. Gomez. 'We can say that.'

They followed him with their gaze, to the distant stairs, where he popped, once, and disappeared, elbows up.

'So,' added Mrs. Gomez, 'it's him or Julio's ash cans.' She paused, over her slicer. 'Or him *and* Julio's ash cans.'

'I can have both?'

'Sure, why not? It's Christmas.'

'Hideous,' said Jeff Beck, watching the Wolf trembling against the Bunny Sisters, the Wolf's snout in their bosom. 'This is a *Christmas* window, you fruitcake.'

'I got carried away,' said Sardos, limp in his director's chair.

'You should be carried away. And plunged in ice water.'

The Bunny Sisters were quivering, the Wolf's paws groping mechanically in their cloaks. Then the Wolf's timer clicked and he fell against them, exhausted.

'Disgusting,' said Beck. He walked over to the Bunny Sisters and disentangled them from the Wolf's paws.

'It was just a momentary inspiration,' said Sardos.

'Is it going to be your *final* inspiration? Or should I plan to spend Christmas morning on this floor?' Beck smoothed the bunnies' cloaks, fluffed up their muffs, straightened their dresses. He turned to Sardos. 'Only a completely depraved person would violate a rabbit.'

'I am that person.' Sardos closed his eyes, sagged deeper into his canvas chair. His unshaven face was haggard, drawn. 'Could I get you to take a look at Pinocchio? I've made some creative adjustments there.' He reached out, clicked Pinocchio's switch.

The card game came on. The skunk brushed her bushy tail across Pinocchio's knees and the enchanted boy's nose came out.

'Oh my god,' said Beck. He walked over to Sardos, leaned over the slouching decorator, lifted him by the lapels. 'They're going to haul you in on a morals charge. Do you understand?' He tapped Sardos lightly on the cheek. 'This window is for *children*. Wee little people. Where do you think you are, on 42nd Street?'

'I was gripped by the myth.'

'You'll be gripped by the vice squad, you slob.' Beck dropped Sardos, back in the chair. 'You'll be run out of town on a rail.'

'Well,' said Sardos, 'isn't that why his nose grew so long? Because he was naughty?'

'Why don't you put a bag of cocaine on his lap while you're at it? Have his nose come in and out of *that*.' Beck opened his tool box. 'But you know—' He buckled on his tool belt. '—I almost don't care anymore. I can always get a job as an unlicensed electrician. Slumlords are looking for people like me.'

'I went over the edge,' said Sardos. 'I see that now.'

Beck picked up a gear wheel from the floor. 'Did this fall out of your head?'

'I don't recognize it as one of mine.'

'Then it must go under here—' Beck lifted the panels beneath the card game and studied the lever-system. '—I'm going to straighten things out in there, and then we're going to pull the curtain.'

'Not yet.' Sardos munched on a candy bar. 'There's one final touch missing.'

'Oh? Did you forget the whip and chain motif?' Beck slid

under the floor, his voice growing fainter. '... *are the Three Little Pigs going to open a massage parlor?*'

Sardos rose slowly from his chair, and knelt by the open floor panels. 'Got any parties lined up for tonight?'

Beck's voice came from underneath. '*Nothing much. I'll probably just go home and soak my head. Have you ever tried that? It clears the mind.*'

'Did you find a present for your aunt?'

Beck's head came out from under the floor. 'I'm giving her electronic football.' He gripped the edge of the panels and crawled back out.

'Have a candy bar,' said Sardos, taking a Mounds bar from his pocket.

Beck looked at it, removed the wrapper. 'From you, Sardos, I expected gourmet chocolate.'

'It was a gift,' said Sardos.

Beck knelt alongside Pinocchio, the length of chocolate in his teeth. 'Alright, we're cleaning up your act.' He slid the enchanted boy away from the skunk's provocative tail, then turned to Sardos. 'And you're going to leave it like this. You're going to leave *everything* as it is.'

'Why?'

'Why? So we can *pull the curtain*. Dann, there is no tomorrow. The store won't even *be open* tomorrow. Christmas is a-comin' in. Do you understand? Or are you too far gone?'

'Probably.' Sardos turned and walked slowly down the Street of the Animals.

MUHLSTOCK WAS waiting, in a little paper hat, below the loudspeaker in the Toy Department. 'ADDEN-SHUN SHOBBERS, DA STORE WILL CLOBE IN FIBDEEN MINUTES. I REPEAB—DA STORE WILL CLOSE IN FIBDEEN MINUTES.'

'Hi,' said Winifred, joining him, a plate of crackers and cheese in her hand, cheese decorated here and there with little pieces of Mrs. Gomez's gauze bandage.

'Lovely,' said Muhlstock, rising on his toes. Then, lowering himself, he flicked a wrist toward a door in the back wall. 'My office ...'

He led her into a small chamber, with desk, filing cabinets, shelves. On the desk was a framed photograph of two little Muhlstocks. On the bulletin board memos hung, precisely pinned, directly through the center. All items in the room had been shown similar attention, everything frighteningly neat. Winifred fought down a mad urge to shuffle it all around, while Muhlstock struggled with a champagne bottle, his grip on the cork compromised by the simultaneous flapping of his elbows. When the cork popped, it struck him between the eyes; he teetered, steadied himself, a red welt forming above his nose. 'Well—' He poured. '—Merry Christmas.'

Winifred pressed her paper cup to his. 'To your beautiful children,' she said, nodding to the studio portrait, in flesh tones so real as to be nauseating, but Winifred's own children had been similarly captured and she was untroubled by the vivid hue. 'They seem so—happy.'

'Yes, that was taken a few months after they left me.'

'I'm sorry.'

'I *tried* to relate to them, I took them to Central Park once a year.' Muhlstock nervously lifted his coned hat, expanding the elastic band upward, then let it snap back down, onto his head. 'I became ill on the carousel.'

'It does go around very fast.'

'You've ridden it?' Muhlstock formed his legs into the number four, one knee bent, ankle up to the opposite knee. Holding this posture, he sat down, a small gain in some ways, Winifred reflected, for his legs were already crossed.

'Yes,' she said, 'I used to take my kids there. I still do, actually. When they're with me.' She sighed into her cup. 'It seems like they've been gone for ages.'

'Mine have been gone for a year,' said Muhlstock. His foot worked up and down on the floor, as if pumping an organ. 'I'd hoped they would miss me, but it seems they prefer my absence.' He lifted his paper cap again, put the band behind his head and shifted the cap to his brow like a horn. 'Is it straight?'

'Perfectly.'

'It feels slightly—off center.' He fiddled nervously with it.

'Allow me, Herb.' Winifred moved the hat around, and settled it back where it had been. 'There.'

'Thank you so much. Neatness—' He stretched his neck, up, up, up, out of his collar, then back down. '—is my passion. But—' He inched the photograph of his children back and forth, tapping it gently on each side. '—perhaps it was a mistake to make my wife line her shoes up every night.'

'Yes,' said Winifred, 'it might've been.'

'She had a great many pairs of shoes.' Muhlstock sipped his champagne. 'What an opportunity she wasted—well, why am I thinking about it now? It's all over, isn't it ...'

'I'm afraid so,' said Winifred.

He looked up at her. 'Yours too? Finished?'

'Completely.'

Muhlstock came out of his chair, legs still shaped in the number four, like a resting water bird. Balancing this way, he grew philosophical. 'We've got to see it through, I suppose. We could put our head in the oven, but it's more sensible to insert a meatloaf. A therapist told me that once. I make a decent meatloaf. You could come over sometime. We could—could watch it bubble through the glass.'

'Sounds like fun,' said Winifred. Sipping her champagne, she thought that perhaps it would be fun, in some distorted way not quite clear to her. Or am I just letting myself in for more heartache? *My* shoes are jammed in closets, drawers, there's one on top of something somewhere ...

She looked at Muhlstock perched in the number four, his eyes darting about like a schizophrenic crane, and tried to imagine such an object around her apartment on a permanent basis.

But, she reminded herself, it's Christmas Eve and Herbert Muhlstock and I are going to spend it alone unless we spend it with each other.

'Yes,' said Muhlstock, 'and I do a thing with canned peaches—' He rolled his tie up on his finger. 'We could—we could do it tomorrow.'

'Ok,' said Winifred, leaning back against his desk. Her feet were killing her; she slipped out of her shoes, and looked at them on the floor, then at Muhlstock. 'Is there any particular way you'd like me to—?'

'No, no, anywhere at all,' said Muhlstock, unrolling his tie.

'I've got to—to live normally, let me—let me just put them over here by the bookcase where they'll be out of our way.'

'Are we going to dance?'

'I'd love to,' said Muhlstock, 'but I never got the hang of it. My tendency is to repeat the first step over and over.'

Winifred wiggled her aching toes inside her stockings, glad of no dancing, relieved in fact that with Herbert Muhlstock one did not have to do any number of things one usually did. She ate a piece of cheese and sipped her champagne, as the department loudspeaker sounded from beyond the door.

'ADDENSHUN SHOBBERS, DA STORE ID NOW CLOBING. DA STORE ID NOW CLOBING.'

'We made it,' said Muhlstock. 'There are No More Shopping Days Until Christmas.' His face twitched into a convulsed smile, lips creased off to the side. 'Some semblance of order will now be restored.' He gestured with his elbow, toward the door and the aisles beyond it. 'I've begun straightening things. The department is mine again, not the horde's.'

'Underneath it all, you really like the Toy Department, don't you,' said Winifred.

'I detest it with every nerve and fiber in my body.' Muhlstock grabbed his nose and rotated it in his fingers, as if, like his conical hat, he might center it more perfectly than nature had chosen to. 'But since I am in it up to my ears, I can at least keep it straight-edged, symmetrically stacked, and *divided ... into ... meaningful ... categories.*' He spoke these last words slowly, as in prayer. Then he pulled his coned hat forward, suspending it ahead of him, in the direction of the door. 'Might we go out now? And gaze at the peaceful aisles?' He traveled toward the extended cone, meeting it with his head again, as if pulled across the room on its elastic. Winifred followed in her stocking feet, champagne cup in hand.

The horde, as Muhlstock had said, was gone. All was empty, save North Pole Headquarters, where one figure remained.

Santa Claus, upon his throne, was gazing out over his snowy yard.

'Poor fellow's exhausted,' said Muhlstock. 'Like the rest of us. He's glad it's over, I'm sure.'

They waved to Santa, and he waved back. Muhlstock then led Winifred over to the electric train layout. 'Shall we?' He opened the gate for her. 'We've got a half hour or so before they lock up.'

Santa Claus watched as the little trains went around in the distance, through their mountain tunnels and over their bridges.

He sighed, started to lift himself off the throne, and sat back down again.

On either side of his throne were elves, their carved forms looking up at him.

'It's all over, boys,' said Santa.

The painted eyes of the elves seemed to blink in the fluttering light that lit the throne. Santa scratched under his beard, his face inflamed. But it was the last night for the old silver whiskers.

He doubted if the job would be his again. Because he kept seeing the blueberry fields when he shut his eyes, and he had a pretty good idea he'd be helping them grow next year, from underneath.

So he was not inclined, just yet, to leave his throne.

He remained in it, thinking about the kids he'd seen today, and yesterday, and all the days. There must have been a million crawled on his lap, and that changes a man inside. Yes, it makes an old tramp think.

He gazed around North Pole Headquarters, at the little house and the dainty reindeer on the roof. The windows were etched with frost and a little fireplace glowed inside. It felt like home, though he'd never slept in it, though the inside was just a mock-up of two-by-fours. And that made you think too.

And the thought was this—that he *was* Santa Claus, that really his life came down to that, for all its roads and sidings, for all its odd-jobs here and there. He was finishing off as Santa Claus, here in the North Pole.

A million kids—he could feel their little hands hanging on to his red suit, and their feet digging in as they climbed up to his knees. And he'd told them about the world, with a pat on the head. You couldn't help but do that, give them what you knew, because it was a fine dust that clings to you and it rubbed off easily onto kids. So they'd taken an old bum's blessing with them, such as it was, and it was anyways a heartfelt wish. What did I travel on for, if not to pick something up as I went and give it away as I could.

A tramp's life isn't worth a dime, so the only gift he's got to give is dust.

The million little hands clung to him, now. He'd already spent his Santa Claus salary but he'd never finish spending what the little hands had bestowed, along with a lollipop in his beard.

Yes, he was Santa Claus, and wasn't that a kicker?

For he strongly suspected that life was dreaming, and what a man dreams he is, that's what he comes down to in the end.

He had the uniform, which is all anyone had ever needed when they'd clapped him in the hoosegow.

The uniform is all you need, and he'd worn it every season for a good many years. He had the whiskers and the big black belt and the nightcap with the pom-pom on it. He and a number of other drifters, ringing bells on street corners, were all of them Santa Claus. That it should be them who took the uniform seemed right, for they were beggars by trade if they had a trade at all, and they could tell the wildest tales ever heard by the north wind. Dreams, yes, lost in dreams, spinning in them, to the end.

He stroked the big wooden arms of the throne; the arc of

little colored bulbs flickered over his head. He wished Christmas would never end, and he'd stay on, taking kids onto his lap, just a good-natured old hobo in a red suit who bounced them up and down on his knee, six days a week, twelve months a year—

—to keep the twinkle in their eyes, and reassure them about certain whispered things. For time would take it from them soon enough, would veil the stars that shone inside them.

He closed his eyes and listened to the faint hum of the reindeers' motor, their delicate legs working around and around, their hooves lightly skimming the roof. He felt himself gliding off with them, into the sky, in his sled full of dreams.

The little hands still clung to him, the little faces still looked into his, little round faces with running noses, and toothless smiles, and cheeks like chipmunks. Gum? He had a beardful.

Candy? He had a couple left.

He opened a little chocolate Santa and popped it in his mouth.

Yessir, that was good liquid to fill a piece of chocolate with. The man who thought of that was a genius.

The rum spilled down his gullet. Reindeer milk that was, to keep Santa's boots up.

He rose slowly from the throne. The soft bulbs continued to wink and blink around him, like the Northern Lights; he'd seen those lights, many times, and known they were his, as much as they were anyone's. Those great lights from the north ridge, high above the lonesome freight—they were the soul of the earth, shining.

And these little lights, winking round his throne, they were the soul of something else, equally hard to define, but real nonetheless, you couldn't tell him different.

For this yard had been packed with kids, who believed in him—who believed what no one else ever had—that he was a good old soul.

He held to the big red cord that lined the walkway down, and gave thanks to the million little travelers who'd let him have that foolish dream, who'd let him believe that his walk on earth had been to good purpose, though much of it had been spent in the ditch.

Ornaments were hanging all around the place. His heart was one too, made of thin glass with snow sprinkled on it.

I'm old, he thought as he walked slowly down the steps. I'm coming round the bend where I always wanted to see, and I'm seeing.

Then he couldn't see anything at all, for the lights in the department had been turned off.

'I've always wondered what this layout looked like in the dark,' said Muhlstock, working his train transformer and watching the headlight of his engine in the hills.

'Enchanting,' said Winifred, sitting beside him, her hand on the other throttle, guiding the illuminated passenger train. She was wearing Muhlstock's engineer cap, balanced on her special holiday hairdo, a little styling she'd given herself in desperation the night before, which made her look like Prince Valiant; Muhlstock's cap covered that, at least, and anyway it was now dark, and she always thought she looked better in complete blackness.

'Herb, I love ... this layout. You did a beautiful job.' She watched her little train winding its way through a plastic village, where every street and sidewalk was laid out with neatly sprinkled rows of colored gravel. The railroad tracks crossed the little roads at perfect intervals, and every house was part of a symmetrical pattern—the whole of it controlled by electric gatemen who came out as the trains passed, swinging their little lighted lanterns.

'Ex-actly on time,' said Muhlstock, checking his watch, as his freight came through.

Switches clicked in the tracks, trains obeyed; gate crossings

128

lowered, and raised, according to plan. Muhlstock oversaw it all, his tics and spasms channeled into the throwing of levers, the guiding of throttles. His eyes traveled beyond the orderly layout, to the aisles of the Toy Department. 'It—' He pointed. '—must run like this. Notice how that far aisle is lining up now? See how everything is in place there, trim as a row of bricks? I spent the afternoon on that.'

Winifred nodded, underneath her cap. She understood. The world of Herbert Muhlstock was not like nature, profuse and wild. It was straight-edged, precise. What was wrong with that?

'My dream,' said Muhlstock, 'is to get everything in boxes. And then put the boxes in boxes.'

He indicated, with another wave of his hand, how orderliness would rule those aisles now shadowy, now darkened. The light of his compulsion would prevail.

His face, suddenly, flew into a vicious tic.

A pair of toy headlights, low to the floor, was coming along the dark aisle. Followed by another pair. And another.

Muhlstock came out from his railroad yard like a projectile, Winifred following.

Muhlstock's elbows began to lower and raise; his right leg came up momentarily into the number four position, then kicked back down.

Battery-powered toy automobiles of every make and shape were coming up the aisle every which way, followed by striding toy robots with rotating heads and blinking eyes. Toy dump trucks were banging around, as were cranes and tractors. An immense traffic jam ensued, cars snarled up, robots falling over them, and tanks crawling over the lot.

A cry of anguish broke from Muhlstock's lips and a series of number fours of the right leg came and went as he hopped forward. A second wave had begun behind the first, little police sirens wailing, tank machine-guns lighting the aisle, sparkling and crackling, along with a wind-up airplane with a fork in its fuselage that caused it to perform a series of roll-overs, round and round.

Following this were a number of small plastic monsters, in various shapes, walking on webbed feet, their tongues spitting fire.

Muhlstock swayed before the tangled maze. His head snapped to the right, toward the next aisle, where new waves could be heard—the entire department marching, rolling, whirring.

'Everything—' he sobbed, '—everything's been opened.'

The first wave of autos had reached him, and an ambulance drove over his shoes. A little plastic monster, eyes mad with sparking fire, was pawing at his cuff. Tanks and police cars closed in around him, and a battery-powered backhoe was digging at his shin.

Muhlstock froze, like an animal paralyzed by highway headlights. He was in number four position, and remained that way, his circuit overloaded. Winifred took his arm. 'Herbert, Herb—' A monster with fins on its back and a low forehead was stroking her stockinged feet, rather affection-ately she thought. But poor Herbert was in shock, teeth clenched, eyes bulging, as if some tremendous tic were about to explode from him but could not. Like a petrified bird, like a stuffed crane, he stood immobile, every feature frozen. Beads of sweat broke out on his brow.

'Herbert, please ...' Winifred removed his conical hat, felt his forehead, as the toys continued on past them, down the aisle, in the direction of Muhlstock's office. Some of them had already reached the back wall, where they buzzed against it, wheels spinning.

'Herbert, we'll put them all back in their boxes. I'll help you. Then we'll put the boxes in boxes—' Winifred tweaked him gently on the cheek, trying to release his frozen grimace.

Suddenly, his number four collapsed, leg coming down, shoe entering the back of a dump truck. He kicked it aside. Body limp, he stared around him at the chaos in the aisle.

'I'm—cured,' he said, voice trembling. He looked down at the little monsters pawing at his cuffs, and at the irregular rows of overturned cars, trucks, planes, robots. He drew his foot slowly back and kicked a plastic dragon up the aisle, its sparking light making a momentary arc before it crashed on the far wall. 'I—don't care!' he cried. 'So what!' he added, raising his arms, above the scattered army of toys.

At the far end of the department, Winifred saw a silver suit ripple, and glide away.

Officer Locke was hidden, in a dog house of rust-resistant aluminum exterior and padded vinyl interior. Through its doorway he commanded a view of the aisles.

I'll get him, thought Locke. He's due here. He starts in Toys, he moves to Sporting Goods, then goes into Hardware.

Locke still had a crick in his neck from the fall he'd taken the other night in Hardware, onto a flying dollie. Another six inches and he'd have rolled right into the elevator shaft.

But I'll get him tonight.

He leaves Hardware and goes through the Pet Department, past Cat Accessories.

Here too, Locke had almost taken a nasty fall in earlier chases, ramming his foot in a litter box and saving himself only at the last moment on a scratching post. Here too, of course, the birds had been loosed—and bird cages had given Locke an idea, about a little cage of his own, a little trap he'd been working on since the lights had gone out.

Louis Fontaine closed his office door and walked down the executive corridor. He stopped before the Accounting Office and looked in. 'You're a bunch of dummies,' he said to the wraiths of his staff. 'You don't know how to handle the IRS. You don't know how to *push*.' He stared at the rows of empty desks. 'You're fired.'

He exited, slamming the door behind him. 'Bunch of college twerps ...' He'd made some money this Christmas, after all. But he'd be giving some of it to the IRS if his accountants didn't do some pushing. 'I want an accountant who's ready to *go to jail*.' He struck a match to his cigar. 'That's the kind of accountant I want.'

He walked down the employee staircase into the store. 'You're beautiful. Fontaine's is the greatest store in America.' His glowing cigar cut through the air. 'With profits like these I can send my wife to the Riviera. And my son to Toe-bending School.' He tapped his ash onto the rug. 'I'll pay for the little nitwit, sure I'll pay, I'm a sucker.' He gazed down the aisle. 'So long as he doesn't bend *my* toes.'

He walked through the hanging yard goods, the finest in the land, his flags of quality. He took an end of some cloth in his fingers. 'This is merchandise.'

The material slipped through his fingers as he walked through the aisle, arm up, stroking each piece. '... lovely stuff, cotton, wool, whatever you want ...' He stroked the last bolt of cloth, and swiveled back around toward it all. 'You want it, you'll find it here, at Fontaine's, a store that's a *store*.'

He walked on, the carpet flowing ahead of him as it had for years, every stitch and corner known to him as few men know even the palm of their own hand.

'It's Christmas Eve, I made a small profit, not much but enough for Toe-bending School.'

He turned into the Fashion wing. The many manikins, each one familiar, stood above him, clad in the advance notices of spring. Fontaine paused beneath them. 'You're looking good. Merry Christmas.' He waved to them. 'Merry Christmas to all the dummies in my store.'

Then, feeling something move behind him, he turned, but saw only a faint wisp of silver pass at the end of the aisle.

Must be one of the birds. He jabbed at the air with his cigar. 'You birds get a bonus. You're good birds. I've got extra seed set out. Stock boys who should be doing other things are feeding you, you're on the payroll.'

He decided to take a swing into the Pet Department, as a good luck gesture. Say Merry Christmas to the hamsters.

One light only shown ahead of him, above the service elevator, the one they were repairing because some moron had rammed into it with a 400-pound rack of paint. Things had been getting badly damaged lately.

Fontaine stepped in front of the half-opened shaft.

'The bottom part of this door is completely dented.' Beneath it were marks Fontaine didn't see, off the wheels of the dollie Locke had ridden full-speed a few nights ago, the 400-pound rack of paint actually Locke's head, which had collided into the door while chasing his quarry.

'The help I've got moving things around these days—' Fontaine shook his head in despair and peered down the shaft, into the darkness, where the ropes disappeared in the depths below. '—however, they got their bonus too. Everybody gets their bonus at Fontaine's. Otherwise—' He relit his cigar and continued on. '—they'd burn the place down.'

He moved along the tiled floor, out of Hardware, and into the Pet Department. 'Now, look, right there, somebody cracked that two-tiered cat post. $39.99 will now become $1.98.'

He peered into a cage of rodents, some kind of little rat that ate a lot of cardboard, a nice pet, take one home, they're on sale. 'How're you doing?' He bent down to their cage. 'Have a nice holiday.'

The rodents ran around, burrowing in their piles of cardboard, and Fontaine walked on. A row of Siamese fighting fish, each in their own bowl, was ahead of him, the fish swirling their long brilliant tails as they swam majestically, and butted at their near brothers, beyond the curving glass of their own bowls.

'How're the fish tonight?' Fontaine watched them swim, a

long shimmering row of them, on sale. 'You're quality fish.'
He bent forward, admiring their swaying fantails.

The fish stared back at him, their eyes flashing. He hunted
along the counter until he found a can of flakes. 'A little bonus
for you too ...' He put a pinch in every bowl and the Siamese
struck upward at the surface. The row livened, swirling fins
flaming in the soft light. Fontaine stepped back, watching with
satisfaction. A row of fish like that—he'd never seen better.

'A nice home awaits you. Every New Yorker needs a fish.'
He shifted his cigar. 'That's not a bad slogan at all. I'll give that
to the Ad Department.'

They rarely took his advice. But what did they know about
selling fish? Nothing.

Fontaine was now standing beside an aluminum dog house.
Within it was Officer Locke.

Locke, however, did not reveal this to his employer.

He felt it might be difficult to explain his presence in the Pet
Department on Christmas Eve. And—the Silver Flash was
due.

Louis Fontaine gazed into a row of empty bird cages.

The best idea some nutty old lady ever had. He'd like to pay
her back. She'd given his Accounting Department something
to add up.

'... here, birdie ...' He called in the darkness.

'... *phreeeeet ... ok Louis* ...'

The bird-voice called from in back of him. He turned,
expecting the bird, but instead there was the silver ripple of a
jogging suit.

'What's that?' Fontaine moved forward. Joggers were crazy,
yes, they sometimes ran in and out of the revolving doors, but
this deep into the store?

He advanced quickly, cigar between his teeth. If somebody
had jogged into the store they would soon be jogging out of the
store—because joggers were not allowed in the aisles. That's
probably how the tennis-wear dummy had gotten cracked, a

jogger had probably run into it. His son was a jogger. Jogged in bare feet, in the snow.

For his toes.

Fontaine swung around the corner, quickly. The silver figure stood in the middle of the aisle, motionless, half-shadow, half-sheen.

'Hey you—' Fontaine moved forward. The silver figure turned quickly, darting off—but Locke jumped out of his dog house, into the aisle.

'Alright, moocher, you're it,' he growled, and moved in.

The Silver Flash darted to the cross aisle, and Locke rumbled after him. The Flash moved with an easy knowledge of the spaces ahead, except Locke had placed a pet enclosure there, of galvanized steel, six feet high and fifteen feet deep, and the Silver Flash had just run into it with a loud clang, followed by another, as Locke whipped the cage door shut behind him.

'Gotcha, hotshot!'

Fontaine was right behind him. 'Locke, what in the name of—'

The Silver Flash stared out through the mesh, fingers gripping the wire. He was a boy. His face was not quite white, and neither was it black. Some Spanish blood flowed through it too, that was clear, from his soft dark eyes and long lashes.

Fontaine peered through the mesh. 'What are you doing in my cage?'

'We got him, sir,' said Locke.

'Got him? What do you mean?'

'He's been hiding in the store.'

Fontaine peered back in. 'Young man—is that true?'

The boy looked up from under his long lashes, dark eyes shifting back and forth nervously from Fontaine to Locke. Finally he nodded, just slightly, to Fontaine.

'You don't have a home?'

The boy stepped back, his movement lithe as a cat's, over the galvanized wire. He went to the door, eyes glancing down at the latch which held him. He turned, paced the other way.

'You can't stay in that cage.' Fontaine gestured with his cigar. 'You're not for sale.'

Locke intervened. 'I'll run him up to the precinct house, Mr. Fontaine.'

'Hold on a moment, Locke. I'll handle this. Young man—' Fontaine turned toward the cage. 'You say you have no home? No family?'

The boy looked at Fontaine; his dark eyes seemed to have lost all boyish innocence, were filled instead with cunning. But this shrewd look passed, dissolving back to childishness, to fear and uncertainty, as he paced in his cage.

Fontaine peered in, closer to the wire. 'Answer me, young man. You have no home? You're free and clear?'

The boy nodded.

'I'm having a great publicity idea, Locke.' Fontaine turned toward his security guard. 'I'll make a media spectacle of this child.' His cigar point was stabbing toward the cage. 'Orphaned youth given a home in Fontaine's Department Store. A charitable deduction and a goodwill image rolled into one. Do you follow me?'

'No sir.'

'That is why you are a security guard, Locke. But you are a good security guard. You have captured, in this galvanized pet enclosure, a million dollar idea.'

'Yessir.'

Fontaine leaned toward the cage again. 'What do you think of that wonderful marketing idea, young man?'

The boy looked at Fontaine, no comprehension in his eyes, a caged creature who was not listening all that closely, attentive to other things—like Locke's hand on the latch.

'Stop prowling in there,' said Fontaine. 'Listen to me—will you do as I say?'

Again the boy's eyes shifted nervously from Fontaine to the cage door, the same mixture of innocence and cunning playing

136

in his gaze, as if he wanted to believe that he was safe with the store owner but could really trust no situation except the darkness in which he knew how to hide.

Fontaine bent toward him. 'Will you? Be a good boy and cooperate?'

The boy nodded.

'Alright, Locke, let him out.'

Locke did so, one of his great meaty paws fastening on the silver cloth at the Flash's shoulder. 'You ain't goin' anywhere, sonny. Got me? Because Mr. Fontaine wants to talk to you.' Locke shook the Silver Flash lightly, giving him a few of the many possible vibrations in his repertoire.

'We'll go downstairs,' said Fontaine. 'My chauffeur will be wanting to go home for Christmas Eve. I'll tell him he can't and then we'll talk some more to this boy. That jogging suit looks familiar. Was it on sale for $29.97?' He turned toward Locke. 'Am I right in assuming this came from a display dummy?'

'Yessir, stripped him naked.'

'Young man, you are fond of that jogging suit?'

Locke, as if translating, shook the question into the boy, whose answer was a quick nod of the head, and then: 'Lemme go, mister. I didn't want to hurt your store. I'll give you back your suit.'

'No, you keep it,' said Fontaine. 'And Monday morning you'll appear in Sportswear, while my Publicity Department photographs the Orphan of the Year.' He looked at the dangling youth. 'Do you know what you are, young man?'

'No.'

'You're a tax shelter.'

Locke stomped along, holding his prisoner in such a way that the boy's sneakers just skimmed the floor, and Fontaine walked beside them, relighting his cigar. 'My Publicity Department will fight me on this, Locke.'

'Yessir.'

'That is because they are out of step with the pulse of this store. This is a store with heart, Locke. People will come here and admire the Orphan of the Year in his new jogging suit.'

Locke shook this information into the boy, who stared at both men fearfully. 'Hey, jus' lemme go, ok? I won't bother your store no more.'

'You're no bother at all, young man. Like the birds, you're on the payroll. And people move up fast in my store. Why? Because I am always firing my executives. You—' He turned, pointed his cigar toward the executive level. '—can go to the top in no time.'

'You ain't gonna put me in Correction?' The boy hung as far away from Locke's grip as he could, head tilted toward Fontaine.

'That's where you belong, you little punk,' said Locke, rattling the Flash. 'But Mr. Fontaine is gonna give you a break.' Locke continued thrashing the boy around at the end of his arm, as if the youth needed his head in motion in order to hear.

In this manner they descended, through the store.

Dann Sardos was alone, walking through the Village of the Animals. The quaint, tilted little houses were snow-covered, cheery. Sardos was morose, gloomy, wondering what to do with the Wolf. Jeff had been right, of course, he could not have the Wolf mashing the Bunny Sisters.

Salvador Dali could. Salvador Dali had pushed a bathtub full of water through Bonwit Teller's window, shattering the glass and dousing the crowd, but, thought Sardos, Dali wasn't working at Bonwit's for a living.

Sardos knelt beside the Wolf and lifted the animal's control panel. It was not the sort of thing you tore apart on Christmas Eve; not without forfeiting your sanity. He paused, gazing at the overturned panel, its nest of wires and mechanical parts.

'... if the Wolf were coming out of the Inn ... I have some room there ...' He hurried to the little Inn, knelt at the miniature door and looked in. '... the Wolf is coming out of the Inn ... loaded ... I'll buckle his knees, drop his cape around him ...'

Behind this sudden flight of imagination, he felt something stonelike in his mind, and recognized it as the bitter truth, that he'd missed his deadline, had a stupid window, and nothing he could do in the next few hours would save him.

The familiar panic swept over him, then the gut-wrenching hunger, then the suicidal despair. He set the Wolf down. '... give me a minute ... I'm oscillating ...'

He sank on both knees in front of the Inn, then slipped forward on his hands and shook his head violently, to clear it, making a gagging sound as he did so. It sometimes helped.

He laid face down in the street, head turned toward the Inn door, as if he himself had just stumbled out of it after a night of carousing with a bunch of rowdy beasts.

Get up, Sardos. You've got to get up.

He was gazing at the Wolf's boots and glistening spurs. An inspiring sight, but he couldn't move. His adrenaline was used up, spent in one panic after another; he'd had it.

Rise, Sardos, rise and shine.

He did not rise and shine; he groped his way through the Inn door, the better to curl up inside it and sleep; sheltered by its snug walls a grown window decorator could feel he'd returned to the womb.

Within the Inn was straw, off in a corner, a pillow for his head. Lying in the straw was a Tootsie Roll.

Sardos stared at it, nested there in the hay.

I am not alone.

He felt, then, the mysterious hand of the unknown friend who'd been sharing these lonely vigils with him. He opened the Tootsie Roll and ate it; a flood of childhood memories came to him, from times he'd forgotten.

He crawled back out of the Inn and stood.

'I have returned.'

He took up his tool kit, brought it to the Inn door. He placed the Wolf on his paws and knees, Wolf crawling through the doorway, cape draped over his ears, only his snout showing. '... the drunken cavalier ... I like it ...' He had room inside the Inn to lay the wires free, let the levers show, then shadow them with the door. The Wolf, his mechanical anatomy designed for walking, would look that much better crawling. He'll look like he *thinks* he's walking. It's pure Cocteau.

Chewing the last of his Tootsie Roll, Sardos looked up at the window in the clouds and whispered thanks again to his secretive companion out there, somewhere in the store.

'*Sardos*!' The voice of Louis Fontaine sounded outside the door.

'Yes, Julius?'

'*Open this door!*'

The doorknob turned; the lock, having already been picked, admitted Fontaine, to the owner's surprise. He stepped into the window area. He was followed by the boy and Officer Locke, who dangled the Flash in over the doorstep.

'Don't try any funny business,' growled Locke. The boy's eyes continued darting around, but he was securely held in Locke's grip.

Fontaine walked through the Village of the Animals. 'Well, well, well ...' His cigar went up and down in his teeth as he admired the village.

'I'm just finishing,' said Sardos, on his hands and knees by the Wolf, head inside the Inn.

'Oh, don't hurry,' said Fontaine. 'Take your time.'

Sardos brought his head out of the Inn and looked up for the first time, to see a young boy dangling from Locke's paw. 'What's going on?'

'This young man in the jogging suit is a homeless boy. He's been living in the store. What I want you to do—' Fontaine paused, puffing on his cigar.

Sardos was swallowing the last of his Tootsie Roll. The boy

was looking at him, a faint smile on his lips, until Locke shook him again, growling, '—*pay attention*—' and lifted him directly between Sardos and Fontaine, where he remained, dangling.

Sardos had the crumpled Tootsie wrapper in his hand. He looked at it, looked at the boy. The boy seemed to give him a nod, or perhaps it was just Officer Locke's paw shaking loose the vertebrae in his neck.

'—what I want you to do,' continued Fontaine, 'is build some kind of charitable display in the center of the store, featuring this boy, who has guaranteed us his full cooperation.' Fontaine looked at the youth. 'Isn't that right?'

The boy's slender form shook all over, collar stretching upward at the end of Locke's arm.

'A cooperative youth who happens to be homeless,' said Fontaine. 'I happen to own a department store. You—' He pointed his cigar at Sardos. '—happen to be my window decorator. We should be able to come up with something.'

'What exactly did you have in mind?' asked Sardos, resuming his work on the Wolf.

'Some sort of tax write-off,' said Fontaine, 'in the name of compassion.'

The boy's head vibrated back and forth, then ceased for a second, as Locke changed hands. Fontaine stabbed the air with his cigar. 'Stop rattling the boy, Locke, he won't be good for anything.'

'Yessir.'

'You're not going to run away, are you, young man?' Fontaine lowered his bushy eyebrows and stared up from under them at the boy.

'N-no,' murmured the boy.

Fontaine indicated with his cigar that Locke should release his captive. this Locke did, reluctantly. The boy took quick glances left and right, toward those hidden passageways he knew of, behind the Village of the Animals.

141

Beyond the village, in the store itself, Santa Claus was making his way along, through the dark aisles; he'd walked the entire store, still in his costume, not wanting to remove it, and knowing he could always slip out through the basement, past the snoring nightwatchman. So he went slowly, floor by floor, until he reached the first floor, and there, seeing the door to the mysterious window ajar, he went up to it and stepped through.

'Good,' said Fontaine, 'here's Santa Claus.' Fontaine peered down the barrel of his cigar toward the suited old drifter, who gazed back in bewilderment through his wig and whiskers.

Fontaine's cigar-tip glowed. 'We have here one runaway boy, and one department store. We're combining them into a message of love and warmth, to be shown daily. Tell me, Santa, right off the top of your head, what strikes you first when you look at this homeless boy, now a member of my firm?'

What struck Santa Claus as he looked at the boy's swarthy face was that he'd seen it a thousand times, across the country and across the years. 'He's familiar.'

'Certainly he's familiar, he's been hiding in the store for weeks.' Fontaine's eyebrows lowered again as he peered at the boy.

Santa's own gaze narrowed, as he saw the windy railroad yards, where kids like this had run faster than any drifter, to grab onto a moving freight. Nowadays they headed for the highway, but it was still the same—this kid was one who takes off young and doesn't come back. 'Yes,' said Santa, 'I've seen him lots of times.'

The boy's eyes widened a little at this, for he'd always moved cautiously round Santa's throne, when he'd slipped through there, when he'd said hello. So how had Santa ever seen him?

Santa blinked behind his wig, and wondered if he was drunker than usual, because he could see the boy's road shining all around him, far into the distance, to lonesome places, ghost towns and chicken shacks, and poverty hollows. He was silvery now, because he was young and fast, and didn't know how the dust finally settles on you and drags your heels. But as sure as he was Santa Claus, this face could be looking out from a doorway someday, gesturing stupidly with a bottle at nothing and no one.

Santa Claus took a step toward him, put his arm around the boy's slender shoulder, which instinctively drew down and away. All you can hope for, thought Santa, is that he sees the fine sunshine on the hills, just once, and it touches him.

'We'll have the tailors make him a number of excellent suits,' said Fontaine. 'Then we'll spotlight him, tastefully, Fontaine's Orphan of the Year. After that, college, Toe-bending School, whatever he wants, so long as he's always wearing an identification tag from the store.' Fontaine paced back and forth. 'The idea will take wings. I have a keen sense about these matters.'

He looked around the Village of the Animals, eyebrows raising as he gazed at it closely for the first time. 'It's good, Sardos. Late, but good.'

Sardos threw the switch that set it all working. The Bunny Sisters gyrated slowly toward Fontaine, their furry bosoms working in and out from gear pins at their waists. 'I like it. It's festive.' Fontaine flicked his ash at the bunnies, then looked at the card-playing dogs.

'What's going on here?' He squatted sideways, checking their cards. The skunk's tail brushed across his knees. 'Play the queen,' he said softly to one of the dogs, and pointed.

The dog's paw moved, elbow clicking, and a card glided on a string into the air, floating there momentarily, and then coming back to the dog's paw.

'There's nothing wrong with this, Sardos. Why haven't you pulled the curtain?'

'I was waiting for you to pull it, Louis,' said Sardos.

Or maybe, thought Santa Claus, as the boy's silver form

whispered in his grasp, maybe he'll see the moon one night over some hidden valley of this land. And the moon will speak to him, as it now and then does, and he'll feel bigger than the entire night.

He shook the boy gently, not as did Locke, but in another way, that of a man who has recently shared his lap with thousands and hundreds of thousands of children—this child's brothers and sisters of the city—

His embrace had a meaning the boy could feel. The boy nodded his head again, as he had to Sardos, almost imperceptibly. An elderly man's aroma of tobacco and rum-chocolate so sweet—this was Santa to him, and he knew the man behind the whiskers was an ok dude.

'That's right, kid,' said Locke. 'You can trust Santa Claus. Every dumbbell in the world knows that.' He rubbed the back of his own neck, where it still hurt from when the little bozo had nearly tumbled him down the elevator shaft. 'And don't forget—guys like me are always waiting for guys like you.' He pointed with his thick finger, into the Flash's chest. 'So stay clean.'

The boy edged slightly away. But he and Locke had played the game, matching steps in the dark. 'How about when I rolled you on that roller skate?' The boy couldn't help but laugh. 'You went sailin', baby ...'

'Champagne, Locke,' said Fontaine. 'Go up to the Liquor Department and bring one of the cheaper cases.' Fontaine turned to Sardos. 'I can't pull your curtain without champagne.'

The door opened and Winifred peeked in. 'Hi, mind if we join the party?'

'Who are you?' asked Fontaine.

'Miracle Filter?' Winifred gestured as if holding a coffee pot.

'Well, Miss Filter, what are you doing in my store at this hour?'

'Excuse me, Mr. Fontaine,' said Muhlstock, stepping forward, 'it's my fault ...'

144

Muhlstock had not been cured as he thought. His cure itself had been only another form of spasm. He once again flapped as he spoke. But he now seemed somehow beyond it.

'Who are you?' Fontaine drew his big gray brows together in a questioning frown, caused by the sight of a man flapping like a chicken in front of him. 'How do you know my name?'

'I work in the store, sir,' said Muhlstock, his voice rising an octave.

'Where, demonstrating Exercycles? Get hold of yourself before you take off.'

'... *ok Louis ... phreeet ...*'

The window in the clouds had opened and Fontaine's parakeet flew in. Fontaine held out his burning cigar but the bird refused it as a perch, and flew on, over Muhlstock's head.

Muhlstock ducked, then snapped into a quick number four, right leg up. 'I'm Herbert Muhlstock,' he said, lowering the leg again. 'I manage the Toy Department.'

Fontaine looked at Muhlstock's feet, to see if the man by any chance were on ball bearings, for he moved back and forth in place faster than any human he'd ever seen. 'You have marvelous energy,' said Fontaine. 'You should be demonstrating—what would you like to demonstrate in my store?'

'Accounting, Mr. Fontaine.'

'No, there can't be anything demonstrated in Accounting. They need quiet. They have to think.' He narrowed his brow again.

'He *is* an accountant,' said Winifred, bringing Muhlstock forward by the elbow.

'Then what,' asked Fontaine, 'is he doing in the Toy Department?'

'I've often asked myself that question,' said Muhlstock.

'Know anything about Charitable Deductions?' asked Fontaine.

'I have near omniscient knowledge on the subject.' Muhlstock brought his coned hat out and in on his forehead.

'We'll have to keep you in the rear of the Accounting Department, Muhlstock, because of your flapping about, but if you know something about Charitable Deductions, the job is yours. I want a good man on that subject.'

'Thank you, sir.' Muhlstock lifted himself up by the lapels, so that he seemed to be held momentarily in traction.

Winifred had moved over beside Santa Claus and the boy in the silver jogging suit. The boy was about the age of her own son, and her lonesomeness came back in a flood. 'Who are you?' she asked.

The boy looked up, dark eyes wary.

'Do you work in the store?'

'He lives in the store,' said Santa Claus, who had lived in some odd places himself.

'You don't have a home?' Winifred put a hand on the young man's arm, and that soft boyish look he returned her made her melt all over. 'You're by yourself at Christmas?'

He moved his head away, with something like a desperate pride, and then she saw a cold mask covering his face.

Tomorrow, thought Winifred, I'll adopt him.

Officer Locke pushed through the door with a case of champagne. The animals in the window were all going, and he had to thread his way through their gyrations. He felt vaguely like arresting the Three Little Pigs. He looked at the Silver Flash. 'You the one put that candy bar in my cap?'

The boy smiled, but one shoulder dropped, snaking down and away from the security guard. Officer Locke, still holding his case of champagne, thrust his head forward. 'I nabbed you anyway,' he said, a glint of victory in his eye. He felt good now; now he'd be able to get some sleep, and not in a standing-up position. Catching the Silver Flash was one of the best Christmas presents he ever gave himself. Locke hoped that if the Flash was going to be on display as an orphan, it'd be in a galvanized pet enclosure with $11\frac{1}{2}$-inch gauge chain links, good strong stuff.

Winifred kept her own light grip on the boy's wrist. '*Did* you put a candy bar in Mr. Locke's cap?'

The boy grinned, and she realized he'd put a candy bar in Muhlstock's cap too, and this way brought her and Muhlstock closer together, a dubious union—but it'd been a lean year and Muhlstock was better than Miltown and manic depression. She watched the boy, who was turning toward the row of houses in the village, his gaze narrowing as he looked at them. His hands were in his back pockets and his head tilted to the side, as if he were trying to see into one of the houses. He has no home, she thought, and even these toy houses look inviting.

Feeling her gaze on him, he turned toward her, and now his grin was a sheepish one, as if he'd felt her reading his mind. Then he slipped his tough mask down, and postured a little, as young boys will, to make it seem that they're equal to any situation.

I'll adopt him first thing Monday morning, thought Winifred.

Locke was popping champagne corks in his massive thumbs, sending them into the painted clouds that floated overhead, the corks falling down and around the assembled employees. Louis Fontaine poured for everyone, including Muhlstock, whose wrist and elbow cranked sideways each time Fontaine tipped the bottle. 'Stop dancing around, Mulesock, this is the finest moderately-priced champagne in the city ...'

'Sorry, sir.' Muhlstock gripped his right hand with his left. 'I've been terribly nervous lately, but I'm getting over it.' He looked toward Winifred, who wondered if Muhlstock's faith in her calming influence was misplaced; she was given to banging on the bathroom wall with her fists and had once, in a mood of despondency, thrown a set of dishes down the air shaft. But that was last Christmas. This was this Christmas. This Christmas would be better. Wouldn't it?

Muhlstock's cup had been filled. He raised it to his employer. 'From the bottom of my heart, Mr. Fontaine, thank you for transferring me to the Accounting Department.'

'Think nothing of it, Mulesock. There's a place for every-one in my firm, even if it's in supply closet, which is where we'll probably have to put you.' He squinted one eye, and watched his accountant bouncing. '... remarkable, simply remarkable ...'

Fontaine turned then, surveying the Village of the Animals, its street and square, its clouds and rooftops, and all its performing inhabitants. He looked at Sardos. 'My Orphan of the Year should be displayed in this window. That'll give some semblance of reason to the public for our delay in opening it. We were waiting for the *right* Orphan of the Year.'

Sardos, having resumed his tinkering, did not seem to hear; it was Christmas Eve, he hadn't bought presents for family, friends, or loved ones, and he was getting an idea for a huge transparent cloth to be lowered around the whole village, to render it more dreamlike and indistinct.

'It's curtain time,' said Louis Fontaine, walking to the corner of the window, where the drawpull hung. He raised his paper cup to his employees, and they raised theirs to him.

'Merry Christmas.'

'Cheers ...'

'Here's luck.'

Fontaine pulled the curtain, and everyone in the window looked toward the glass.

Mad Aggie was looking back through it.

'A nutty old woman,' said Fontaine, peering down at the bag-lady. He turned toward his security guard. 'Officer Locke, I believe this to be the woman who let my parakeets loose—one of the finest marketing moves of my career. Since it is Christmas Eve, I wish to give her something of equal value, in return. Go out at once and give her two new shopping bags.'

Aggie, face against the glass, stood in the cold wind of the avenue. Newspapers blew against her ankles, and the window echoed with music from loudspeakers overhead.

'... *come and behold Him, born the King of an-gels ...*'

Dark space had opened before her eyes, to another dimension. In its center stood a child made of silver. Around his head was a halo of moonlight, rays shining outward, with music sounding all around him.

'... *oh come let us a-dore Him ...*'

He looked at her, his eyes flashing diamonds. The light sizzled into her with a buzzing sound that crackled all through her addled head.

'... *oh come let us a-dore Him ...*'

His silver form grew brighter, lighting up all over, and Aggie saw great moons in strange clouds above him, moons of the far night shining, burning, striking her all over with their beams.

The dark angels of the canyon swooped down and hovered over her. Then they dropped upon her, wrenching and dividing her, into three. *You're the Magi, Aggie. You come bearing gifts ...*

Against her will, her arms started to lift upward, toward the radiant child of the lost dimension. To her horror, her fingers started to unbend from the cord handles of her shopping bags.

Present your gifts, Aggie, whispered the dark angels, *present them to the Prince of Peace.*

She struggled to hang on to them, she needed those shopping bags for anchors, needed the handles to hang on to, for they were the only grip she had on the swirling night. '... no ... get away ...'

She tried to close her fingers back up, but they were loosening anyway, and her arms were still raising upwards, until her bags were held out to the silver child, and she lost her grip on them.

The dark angels laughed, crying, *the gift has been made,* and her bags fell to the sidewalk at the base of the window to the lost dimension.

Within the dimension, the child's form flashed again, and

the crackling sound spiraled through her ears and down inside her. The kid was moving, in back of some other people in the glass world beyond her—he was slipping behind them, his form smooth and slippery as milk from the moonplant. He was slipping into some cockeyed houses they had there, his light blazing through the windows. He stood inside one of the houses for a moment, shining, and then he was gone.

A door opened to the street, and Officer Locke stepped out.

Aggie stared at him, up through her blowing gray hair. She'd dropped her shopping bags, lost her grip, and now they were arresting her. She held her gnarled hands out to be handcuffed, her fingers bent as if her precious cord-handles still hung there.

'Here you go, lady—' Locke bent down, picked up her old shopping bags and dropped them into some new ones. He hung them onto her outstretched hands. 'Merry Christmas from Mr. Fontaine.'

'Thanks, George,' said Aggie, staring at the brilliant sheen of the new bags, and at the jowled face of Officer Locke.

Locke nodded, satisfied that his assignment had been carried out, then watched to see that the old doll didn't try to sneak into his store. That's all he needed, along with everything else he'd been through lately.

'You look tired, George,' said Aggie.

'Just keep movin' . . .'

Aggie pushed on, up the street. Her bags were shining and her handles had been doubled, two loops of cord in each hand, four good strong grips on the moon.

The wind blew against her, but she had the anchors dragging, bright new ones.

She turned the corner and saw the silver child slipping out the side door of the canyon. 'Hey!' yelled Aggie.

The boy turned. His slender body crackled with moonfire and snowflakes came out of his fingertips as he waved to her. She waved back and slushed up to him, to where he was standing nervous as a silver cat, looking both ways on the street, and taking a big drink of air, a sigh like Aggie always took, the one that got you going. He's just like me, she thought, and gave him a wink.

'You got any insulation in that jacket?' She pointed at his thin silver suit, then rummaged in her bag, bringing out some thick newspaper, the kind that made you feel you were lined with wool. 'Take this, stuff it in your pants, and take this one—' She yanked another folded newspaper out. '—put this in your jacket, over your chest.'

The boy took the papers reluctantly, but then opened his silvery jacket.

'That's it, Tommy, you stay insulated and you'll do alright on the moon.'

He zipped his jacket around the padding, and then his face softened for a moment, and he pointed to Aggie's bulging coat. 'You all newspaper?'

Aggie patted her bulging coat. 'Every last bit of me.'

He smiled a faint silver smile. 'I got to go now.'

'Sure you do. You run along and play, Tommy. But be home for supper. I'll make something nice for you.'

The boy gazed at her, through the mist of his own direction. 'Yeah, ok,' he said, backing slowly away.

'Hey!' She rammed her hand back in her bag and brought out the flattened egg sandwhich. 'You take this, for later. In case you're playin' somewhere and you get hungry.' Her palm was out, the sandwich in it. 'The King of the Moon ran over it.' She shoved it closer to him.

'You keep it,' said the boy, and folded her gnarled old fingers back around it.

She saw his eyes flashing silver, the cold edge of what he followed. 'Alright, run along ...' She lifted her bags, and watched him go, off down the block.

He's a good boy, thought Aggie, shuffling slowly after him, head pulled down into her shell, and he running ahead like a silver hare, his slender body crackling with moonfire.

He'll make out fine, she thought. I might have made a few mistakes bringing him up but he knows his way around the moon.

His silver figure drifted sideways as he jogged, and then suddenly he darted, and disappeared. Aggie nodded, and followed slowly after him, galoshes slapping through the gray melting snow, to the intersection.

She whirled around, her bags up. The buildings sped by her in a ring; she spun to a stop, nose pointed.

She crossed the intersection, her small shuffling form slowly reaching the other side, and then as slowly disappearing, up the long avenue.

The wind blew along it, rattling awnings, whispering through the few slender trees. Of the department stores that formed the dark avenue, only Fontaine's still showed signs of life.

There, in a window, the small party continued, hosted by Louis Fontaine, who'd just lost the worst marketing idea of the year. He chewed on his cigar, thinking up new ones.

Beside him stood Herbert Muhlstock, twitching, but looking forward to Monday morning in the Accounting Department. Does his hope lie there? Not even Muhlstock thinks so. But there he will be, chewing the heads off erasers. His photo of the little Muhlstocks will be before him. With a suitable chaperon, approved by the court, he will be able to visit them sometime soon.

He turned toward Winifred Ingram, and she toward him. Their paper cups touched. She was wearing a railroader's cap, and knew, after all, that Muhlstock wasn't the man, nor was this window the place, but she was halfway through the night and survival until morning now seemed a distinct possibility, and she dared not ask for more in her Christmas stocking, for that was enough.

Beside her, drinking all the champagne he could, was a rum-filled Santa Claus. Upon him was the imprint of a hundred-thousand little hands, an imprint already fading, for with Christmas morning Santa's work is done. But—he raised the cup to his lips—any year that found a man topside of a ditch was a good one.

Officer Locke, drinking next to him, was also satisfied. He had gotten his man, even though his man had already escaped again. But that wasn't his fault. If management wanted to let kids out of galvanized pet enclosures to run around free, that was their business, not his. He was smoking a good cigar. When it became gray ash he would call it a night and go to his room on Ninth Avenue, where he would spend the holiday in bed instead of in an aluminum dog house.

As for Dann Sardos, he was trying to hang diaphanous cloth, suggestive of dreams. The window and the city, he knew, were bride and groom, for better or worse. He stood on the rung of a ladder, arms above him, adjusting some hooks for the fabric. The party continued below him. As parties go, it was one of the better ones he'd attended on the dreadful Eve, for it was, as the good ones always were, an accident, and the folks attending it bound by the merest of threads. Looking out through his window, he could not help feeling that the city and perhaps the earth itself hung by his fine thread, woven between strangers.

TIME AFTER TIME

Molly Keane

Bestselling author of Booker Prize runner-up
GOOD BEHAVIOUR

The ageing, one-eyed Jasper Swift and his three grotesque, elderly
sisters, April, May and Baby June, have been waging quiet guerilla
warfare against one another for years. They live together in damp,
decaying Durraghglass, the country estate left to them all by darling
Mummie.

Then, suddenly, their long-lost cousin returns from Vienna. Exotic
Leda, whom Daddy had been so funny about all those years ago; and
within days, the uneasy existence of the Swifts has been dramatically
overturned, when desires, dormant for so long, flame fierce and bright
as ever . . .

Poignant and hilarious, controlled yet outrageous, TIME AFTER
TIME brilliantly captures the graceless setting of the sun on the
eccentric Anglo-Irish aristocracy, emulating the classic comedy of
Molly Keane's acclaimed novel GOOD BEHAVIOUR.

'Vivid and graceful . . . it is a joy to read.' *Spectator.*
'Sharp, deadly and irresistibly funny.' *Daily Telegraph.*
'The pleasure in grotesqueries is as gleeful as ever.' *Observer.*

FICTION   0 349 12076 5   £2.95

A Hot Country

SHIVA NAIPAUL

Award-winning author of Fireflies *and* The Chip-Chip Gatherers.

In Cuyama, a simmering corner of South America, the era of the humane intellectual is over. A blacker, more brutal age is about to begin and nobody outside the country's own borders will very much care. Yet, through the anguished lives of those who are marooned there – aristocratic bookshop owner Aubrey St. Pierre and his wife Dina – we are drawn into the turmoil of the impending plebiscite in post-Independence Cuyama, nakedly addressing the fear of chaos, the breakdown of order, moral decline and decadence, in a disturbing and brilliant exposure of the corruption of colonialism and the horrors of a decolonised future . . .

A HOT COUNTRY marks Shiva Naipaul's outstanding return to fiction, after a ten year silence; written with haunting lyricism and powerful precision, its poignant themes of loss, displacement and yearning are universal.

'A work of art that delights with its craft as it dismays with its vision.' *Times Literary Supplement*.

'A far finer achievement than [Salman Rushdie's] Shame.' *The Scotsman*.

'A book of great power.' *Daily Telegraph*.

FICTION   0 349 12492 2   £2.95

Also by Shiva Naipaul in Abacus paperback:

BLACK AND WHITE

Also available in ABACUS paperback:

FICTION

TIME AND THE HUNTER	Italo Calvino	£2.50 ☐
THE LOST VILLAGE	David Glover	£2.50 ☐
WHAT A BEAUTIFUL SUNDAY!	Jorge Semprun	£2.95 ☐
BETHANY	Anita Mason	£2.95 ☐
A HOT COUNTRY	Shiva Naipaul	£2.95 ☐
THE KING DAVID REPORT	Stefan Heym	£3.50 ☐
THE ISSA VALLEY	Czeslaw Milosz	£3.25 ☐
TIME AFTER TIME	Molly Keane	£2.95 ☐
I HEAR VOICES	Paul Ableman	£2.50 ☐
BREAKFAST AT TIFFANY'S	Truman Capote	£1.95 ☐

NON-FICTION

THE GREAT EVOLUTION MYSTERY	Gordon Rattray Taylor	£3.95 ☐
IRISH JOURNAL	Heinrich Böll	£1.95 ☐
THE SECOND STAGE	Betty Friedan	£2.95 ☐
IRELAND – A HISTORY	Robert Kee	£5.95 ☐
TERRORISM	Walter Laqueur	£2.75 ☐
THE BAD BOHEMIAN	Sir Cecil Parrott	£2.95 ☐
HITCH	John Russell Taylor	£2.75 ☐
THE ROBOT AGE	Peter Marsh	£2.95 ☐
MRS HARRIS	Diana Trilling	£2.95 ☐
THE STRENGTH TO DREAM	Colin Wilson	£2.95 ☐

All Abacus books are available at your local bookshop or newsagent, or can be ordered direct from the publisher. Just tick the titles you want and fill in the form below.

Name _____

Address _____

Write to Abacus Books, Cash Sales Department, P.O. Box 11, Falmouth, Cornwall TR10 9EN

Please enclose cheque or postal order to the value of the cover price plus:

UK: 45p for the first book plus 20p for the second book and 14p for each additional book ordered to a maximum charge of £1.63.

OVERSEAS: 75p for the first book plus 21p per copy for each additional book.

BFPO & EIRE: 45p for the first book, 20p for the second book plus 14p per copy for the next 7 books, thereafter 8p per book.

Abacus Books reserve the right to show new retail prices on covers which may differ from those previously advertised in the text or elsewhere, and to increase postal rates in accordance with the PO.